The Report of the LAMBETH CONFERENCE 1978

CIO Publishing
London

ISBN 0 7151 4563 0

First published in 1978 by Church Information Office

Made and printed in Great Britain by Bocardo & Church Army Press Ltd., Oxford

Contents

The authority of this report

The resolutions are resolutions of the whole Lambeth Conference in plenary session, taken by a vote of bishops. Consultants, observers, and clerical and lay members of the Anglican Consultative Council did not vote, though they were invited to contribute freely to the debates. Voting was by show of hands, and resolutions were accepted on a simple majority of bishops present and voting. Numbers of votes and abstentions were only recorded in the case of resolution 21. The resolutions have no legislative authority unless or until they have been accepted by the Synods or other governing bodies of the member Churches of the Anglican Communion, and then only in those member Churches.

In the case of Section 1, what is here presented is an editorial collation of views expressed in the course of discussion by the section and in its groups during the Conference; the reports of Sections 2 and 3 have the authority of their respective sections.

The speeches in the Appendix give the personal opinions of those who delivered them. The Steering Committee asked that they be printed here, without implying that the Conference is committed to their contents.

The chapter 'The Life of the Conference' and the reports of the Hearings are the work of the General Editor, at the request of the Steering Committee.

The life of the Conference

The eleventh Lambeth Conference was unlike its predecessors in a number of ways. For a start, it was residential, and held outside London—in the University of Kent at Canterbury. Because we shared our daily worship, our meals, and our leisure as well as our business, it was possible to become aware as never before of the Anglican Communion as people rather than as entries in a Yearbook or Directory. The hopes and fears and plans of other Churches of our Communion became the hopes and fears and plans of people whom we met day by day. The old world, the new world, and the third world were known—by experience—to be one in Christ. The theme of the Conference was 'Today's Church and Today's World', with a special focus on the ministry of bishops. The fact that it lasted only three weeks—a much shorter time than any recent Lambeth Conference—meant that there was not the time to write long reports and debate a plethora of resolutions in plenary sessions. In the event, the Conference passed only 37 resolutions, compared with the 69 of 1968 and the 131 of 1958. This was deliberate; much more time was spent in small groups of a dozen or twenty, in which it was possible for more Conference members to make their contribution to what was finally expressed as the mind of the Conference, and to have that person-to-person, mind-to-mind, soul-to-soul interaction which made 'Lambeth 1978' so memorable an experience for everyone who took part.

The plenary sessions and decisions of the last few days of the Conference were therefore the culmination of a time of gradual preparation in which the bishops (and their consultants, observers from other Churches, and selected clerical and lay members of the Anglican Consultative Council, all of whom took a full and active part, even if they did not have voting rights) could be sensitized both to the vortex of political events and economic forces in the world outside, and to the voice of God. We were repeatedly reminded that God often speaks to his Church through that vortex and within the material and human world of which he is the creator and where he reigns—whether we hear or whether we disobey, whether we decide wisely or whether we decide foolishly. To that end the Conference was addressed, towards the beginning of its sessions, by Lady Jackson (Barbara Ward, the economist) and the Reverend Charles Elliott, Professor of Development Policy and Planning at the University of Wales.

Lady Jackson's lecture on 'The Conserving Society' reminded us that for the first time in history, we could create a planetary society in which all men enjoyed dignity and freedom; but the interdependence of our limited natural resources was such that we lived in a state of fragility in which exploitation of a part could destroy the balance of the whole instead of leading the world to its Utopia. Professor Elliott, speaking on 'Economics and Choice—The Crucial Battleground', showed how the balance of economic forces was working in such a way that the rich were becoming still richer at the expense of the poor. The biggest failure of communication in the world today was that between the technician and the visionary. It was fundamentally an ethical issue to see that the discoveries of technology were used to the benefit of Christ's poor and not to titillate the jaded palates of that tiny proportion of the world's population who could afford to have jaded palates.

This sensitivity to the needs of the world and the cries of Christ's poor did not mean, as some sections of the Press were suggesting, that the bishops were so immersed in worldly affairs that they forgot to listen to God's still small voice. Rather the opposite. The Conference was enfolded within worship. Each day began with the Eucharist and the daily Office, celebrated in the same hall where the plenary sessions took place, and taken in turn (and sometimes in more than one language) by a different Province of the Anglican Communion. The Conference owed much, more than it perhaps realized, to the unobtrusive presence of Bishop Edward Roberts (formerly Bishop of Ely) who acted as its Chaplain throughout.

Immediately after breakfast each weekday, there was a devotional lecture. Metropolitan Anthony of Sourozh (known to many as Archbishop Anthony Bloom) delivered these during the first week, when he also conducted a Quiet Day for the whole Conference. The firm authority of his deep spirituality set us all in the right framework for our debates and discussions. The risen Jesus, at the end of the Gospel narrative, told his disciples to go back to Galilee and meet him there. Galilee was the place where they had first met him, in that spring-time when all things were new and all things were possible. Metropolitan Anthony called us back to our Galilee—back to our Christian beginnings, when we were not ecclesiastical professionals, when we were not public figures, when we had no appearances to keep up, but only reality to know—when we were growing with joy and amazement into the new discovery of God's world and word and kingdom and person.

The devotional addresses in the second week were given by the Reverend Christopher Duraisingh of the Church of South India, who gave us a series of Bible studies on the temptations of Jesus, which were his period of preparation and discernment as he struggled 'to get the accent in the right place' in his mission and ministry. So we stood with him in the wilderness, at the threshold of new decisions, constrained by the Spirit and set between God and the plausible devil, praying for the gift of spiritual discernment as we sought to learn the shape of our so vulnerable ministry.

Archbishop Stuart Blanch of York gave the third and final series of lectures when with his inimitable fund of good humour employed to help us realize deep spiritual truths, he took us on a tour of Canterbury and the Conference in the company of St Irenaeus. Irenaeus lived in the days when the Church was young. He was a bishop in a squalid little town on the outposts of empire, with a mere handful of clergy, in an unpredictable totalitarian state, at the mercy of its every whim. His Church, beset by false teachers, when neither orthodoxy nor heresy had been clearly defined, was a small and feeble thing; his congregations were tiny and his diocese contemptible. But he had an unerring instinct for the essential—for union with Christ the Word made flesh, in his manhood, his sufferings, his victory, and his vision. Irenaeus, being dead, spoke livingly to us at Lambeth 1978.

In their very different ways, the three series of devotional lectures reminded us, not only of our need to remain sensitive to God, but of the ecumenical and international dimensions of Christian spirituality. That also came home to us when Pope Paul VI died and the Roman Catholic observers were invited to celebrate a Requiem Mass in the plenary hall. Two of the lessons were read by Bishop Howe and by Archbishop George Simms of Armagh.

There were also the great moments of worship at the beginning and end of the Conference and on the London day. At the opening Eucharist in Canterbury Cathedral on 23rd July, Archbishop Sepeku of Tanzania presided, the Archbishop of Canterbury preached, and music was provided not only by the choir and organist of the Cathedral but by the Groovers Steel Orchestra who helped us to rejoice in the Lord with truly West Indian verve and panache. There was the splendour of Festal Evensong at Westminster Abbey on 1st August with Archbishop Moses Scott of West Africa preaching, and the closing Sung Eucharist at Canterbury on 13th August, when the chief celebrant was the Archbishop of Canterbury, the sermon was preached by Presiding Bishop John Allin of the Episcopal Church in the U.S.A., and a chapel in the Cathedral was dedicated in memory of twentieth-century saints and martyrs. Also in Canterbury Cathedral, on 30th July, a chapel was dedicated to the memory of Archbishop Geoffrey Fisher, the President of the Lambeth Conferences of 1948 and 1958. We are grateful to the Deans and Chapters of Canterbury and Westminster for the arrangements they made for all these occasions.

Messages of greeting were received at the opening of the Conference from the General Secretary of the Lutheran World Federation, the President and Secretary of the World Alliance of Reformed Churches, the Chairman of the Conference of Secretaries of the World Confessional Families, the Chairman and General Secretary of the World Methodist Council, His Holiness Pope Paul VI, the Cardinal Archbishop of Westminster, the General Secretary of the World Council of Churches, and the Patriarch of Moscow and All Russia. During the Conference we heard a tape-recorded message of greeting from Archbishop John Aung Hla of Burma, who was unable to attend.

The University of Kent at Canterbury held a Special Congregation in the nave of the Cathedral on 26th July, when the degree of Doctor of Civil Law was bestowed, *honoris causa,* by the Chancellor of the University, the Rt Hon. Jo Grimond, M.P., on three representative members of the Conference: Bishop John Coburn of Massachusetts, Archbishop George Simms of Armagh, and Bishop Desmond Tutu, General Secretary of the South African Council of Churches. Those who were present will not readily forget the speeches of Professor Hagenbuch, the acting Public Orator, or the address by the Vice-Chancellor (Dr Geoffrey Templeman) in which he reminded us of Anselm, that great mediaeval Archbishop of Canterbury, and the abiding truth of his conviction that true religion and sound learning are each impoverished if they neglect the other.

On Friday, 28th July Mr Alec McCowen, the actor, gave a special performance of his solo recital of the whole of the Gospel according to St Mark in the Authorized (King James) Version, for bishops and their wives. Many must have found that Gospel coming alive for them in a totally fresh way through this experience. During the Conference the Guildford Philharmonic Orchestra gave a concert in the Cathedral and the Royal Shakespeare Company presented *Twelfth Night* and Chekhov's *Three Sisters* in the Gulbenkian Theatre of the University. On a lighter note, there was a cricket match on the campus on Saturday, 29th July between the bishops and a local team led by the Reverend J. C. Meek, Rural Dean of Canterbury. The Conference upheld the honour of the episcopate by scoring 152 for 4 as their reply to 141 for 6 declared. Excursions to local places of interest were arranged for the two Sundays.

As has already been mentioned, 1st August was the London day. The entire Conference was received at Lambeth Palace by Archbishop and Mrs Coggan, toured the Palace and grounds, and had lunch in and around a marquee in the gardens. Festal Evensong followed in Westminster Abbey and then—with the clouds gathering but the rain of the English summer miraculously still holding off—the Conference had the honour of being received at Buckingham Palace for an afternoon Garden Party. Her Majesty the Queen was absent in Canada, so Queen Elizabeth the Queen Mother graciously acted on her behalf. The Princess Margaret, Countess of Snowdon, Princess Alice, Duchess of Gloucester, and the Duchess of Kent were present. The Queen's Bodyguard of the Yeomen of the Guard were on duty and the band of the Scots Guards played selections of music—including, to the delight of many, 'Consider yourself at home; Consider yourself one of the family'. We were made so relaxedly welcome that it seemed true. Another civic occasion took place at the end of the Conference, on 13th

August, when the Mayor and Mayoress of Canterbury received all of us at an afternoon Garden Party and tea at Tower House, which ended by everyone (led by Archbishop Coggan) singing 'Auld Lang Syne' with linked arms.

During the last week of the Conference, Mrs Coggan arranged a separate Conference at Christ Church College, Canterbury, for bishops' wives, which was attended by over 230 of them from all parts of the world. Bishop Lesslie Newbigin led a Quiet Day and there were daily group meditations. Dr Jack Dominian spoke on marriage and Dr Cicely Saunders on bereavement, and there was a panel of speakers on different aspects of women's ministry in the Church. There were practical workshops on 'communication', radio through television, and script-writing for the Press; and outings and entertainment. Bishop Stephen Verney took an Epilogue on most evenings, and the Archbishop of Canterbury celebrated Holy Communion one morning, stayed for breakfast and then spoke to the wives on some of the issues that were before their husbands that week.

What of the business of the Conference? The rest of this volume contains the result of it. There were three sections and 34 small groups in each of which particular areas of concern could be worked at in the privacy of intimate discussion. Bishops had indicated their group preference and been allocated to groups 9 months before the Conference took place, and each participant had been sent a volume of Preparatory Essays, so that group discussion could be well prepared and well-informed. In addition, twelve regional groupings met at least twice during the Conference. Their purpose was to enable concerns of a particular part of the globe to be ventilated in such a way that they could affect the deliberations of all relevant groups and sections, and the eventual resolutions of the whole Conference. It was in this way, for example, that resolution 3 arose—first as a concern of the bishops of Africa, then re-expressed as a matter of universal import.

Sections, regional groupings, and groups met in private. Only the plenary sessions were open to the Press, and accredited members of the Press from all over the world were present in the gallery on these occasions. A few bishops addressed these sessions through interpreters, and there were facilities for simultaneous translation of plenary sessions, by volunteers using the 'whisper' method to a little knot of people, into French, Japanese, Korean, and a Rwanda/Burundi vernacular. Our thanks go to all those who made this possible.

The four Hearings were plenary sessions. These were not debates, but opportunities for individual Conference members to offer information and put points of view before the full Conference on four areas of concern for the Anglican Communion as a whole, so that groups and sections could incorporate them into their thinking at a time when their reports were still in an embryonic state.

The voting strength of the Conference consisted of the bishops alone—407 of them, mainly diocesans, but with a sprinkling of coadjutors, suffragans, and assistant bishops. Clerical and lay members of the ACC, consultants, and observers from other Churches took an active part in all debates and discussions but did not vote. There is a statement on p. 5 about the authority of various portions of this report.

If we were to start expressing our thanks to those who have helped the Conference in any way, the list would be an impossibly long one—but a special word of gratitude must go to the indefatigable Miss Pamela Bird, who has for fourteen years been personal secretary, first to Bishop Dean and then to Bishop Howe, and is about to return to Canada to work in Church House, Toronto. Her tiny band of dedicated office staff worked constantly and uncomplainingly throughout the entire Conference, often far into the night, typing, copying, and duplicating drafts and documents. The weight of paper consumed by the Conference in three weeks ran to several tons. Perhaps each bishop, on his return, would undertake to plant a tree in reparation?

This chapter has been entitled 'The Life of the Conference', but a bald recital like this cannot do anything remotely like justice to that life. The Conference *was* alive. Not once but twice it took the planned programme and remade it, because things were working out in a different way than could have been foreseen in advance and apart from the living forces which were shaping its work and progress. The fact that the Conference was residential meant that it was so much more natural and easy for old friendships to be cemented and new ones to be forged. The fellowship that was experienced at Canterbury in the summer of 1978 has resulted in greater gains for the Anglican Communion and its bishops than a cold recital of the resolutions or a reading of the reports can convey. We owe a great debt of gratitude to the staff of the University, whose unfailing courtesy and helpfulness enabled the Conference to run smoothly and happily. But our final words of thankfulness must be to almighty God. After the final plenary session, when the Archbishop of Canterbury had given us his blessing, the whole Conference spontaneously broke out into the singing of 'Praise God, from whom all blessings flow; and that evening many of the bishops and their wives and friends met together in the plenary hall for a time of prayer and praise, and heard witnesses from many parts of the world telling them some of the wonderful things God has been doing through his Church in our days. That same God has, we believe, richly used our three weeks together at the Lambeth Conference of 1978 in ways and for purposes which only the years ahead will unfold. To him be the glory for ever! Amen.

Officers of the Conference

President
F. D. Coggan
Archbishop of Canterbury

Secretary
John Howe
Secretary General of the Anglican Consultative Council

General Editor
Michael Perry
Archdeacon of Durham

Chaplain
E. J. K. Roberts
Formerly Bishop of Ely

Steering Committee

John Howe	Secretary General of the Anglican Consultative Council *Chairman*
F. D. Coggan	Archbishop of Canterbury
D. M. Tutu	Assistant Bishop in the Province of South Africa General Secretary of the South African Council of Churches Chairman of Section 1
G. O. Simms	Archbishop of Armagh and Primate of All Ireland Vice-Chairman of Section 1
J. S. Kingsnorth	Honorary Canon of Lusaka Deputy Secretary and Editor, United Society for the Propagation of the Gospel Secretary of Section 1
D. W. Hambidge	Bishop of Caledonia, Canada Chairman of Section 2
M. N. C. O. Scott	Archbishop of West Africa Vice-Chairman of Section 2

Austin Masters	Priest of the Society of the Sacred Mission Diocesan Missioner and Ecumenical Officer, Diocese of Exeter Secretary of Section 2
P. C. Rodger	Bishop of Manchester Bishop-elect of Oxford Chairman of Section 3
A. H. Johnston	Archbishop of New Zealand Vice-Chairman of Section 3
E. S. Light	Archdeacon of Saskatchewan General Secretary of the General Synod of the Anglican Church of Canada Secretary of Section 3
Michael Perry	Archdeacon of Durham *Secretary*

The Steering Committee was for the day-by-day work of the Conference.

Primates Committee

The Archbishop of Canterbury	*Chairman*
Archbishop Marcus Loane	Australia
Archbishop Arthur Kratz	Brazil
Archbishop John Aung Hla	Burma (absent)
Archbishop Edward Scott	Canada
Archbishop Donald Arden	Central Africa
Bishop Gilbert Baker	China
Archbishop Trevor Huddleston	Indian Ocean
Archbishop George Simms	Ireland
Bishop Samuel Imai	for Primate of Japan
Bishop Hassan Dehqani-Tafti	President Bishop, Jerusalem and the Middle East
Archbishop Festo Olang'	Kenya
Archbishop Norman Palmer	Melanesia
Archbishop Allen Johnston	New Zealand
Archbishop David Hand	Papua New Guinea
Bishop Alastair Haggart	Primus of Scotland
Archbishop Bill Burnett	South Africa
Bishop Colin Bazley	President of CASA (South America) (absent)

Archbishop Elinana Ngalamu	Sudan
Archbishop John Sepeku	Tanzania
Archbishop Silvanus Wani	Uganda, Rwanda, Burundi, and Boga-Zaire
Bishop John M. Allin	Presiding Bishop, U.S.A.
Archbishop Gwilym Williams	Wales
Archbishop Moses Scott	West Africa
Archbishop Alan Knight	West Indies
Bishop John Howe	Secretary General of the Anglican Consultative Council *Secretary*

The Primates Committee was convened for major decisions about the Lambeth Conference, and for some matters concerning Regional Sessions and unassigned Plenaries; and for subjects on which the Archbishop of Canterbury wished to seek the Committee's views.

Participants

Bishops

Note:
In the first column, the word 'assistants' includes suffragan, coadjutor, and assistant bishops from the Province concerned. The first digit in the final column indicates the section (1, 2, or 3) to which the bishop was assigned, and the figure as a whole is that of his group. A list of sections and groups is to be found on pages 28–29 below. The chairman of a group is indicated by the letter C after his group number and the secretary by the letter S. Chairmen, Vice-chairmen and Secretaries of sections are members of the Steering Committee and are listed on pages 12–13 and 28–29.

Archbishop of Canterbury	F. D. Coggan	—
Secretary	J. W. A. Howe	—
Church of England in Australia		
Adelaide	K. Rayner (Abp)	110
Armidale	P. Chiswell	103
Ballarat	J. Hazlewood	202
Bathurst	E. K. Leslie	212
Bendigo	O. S. Heyward	101 C
Brisbane	F. R. Arnott (Abp)	304
Bunbury	A. S. Goldsworthy	109
Canberra and Goulburn	C. A. Warren	210 S
Carpentaria	H. T. Jamieson	201
Gippsland	G. R. Delbridge	303 C
Grafton	D. N. Shearman	307
Melbourne	R. W. Dann (Abp)	102
The Murray	R. G. Porter	206
Newcastle, NSW	A. C. Holland	207
North Queensland	H. J. Lewis	203; 213 S
Northern Territory	K. B. Mason	105 C
North West Australia	H. A. J. Witt	104 S
Perth	G. T. Sambell (Abp)	205
Riverina	B. R. Hunter	208 S
Rockhampton	J. B. R. Grindrod	211; 213
Sydney	M. L. Loane (Abp)	106
Tasmania	R. E. Davies	209 S

Wangaratta	M. M. Thomas	108
Willochra	S. B. Rosier	111 C
Assistants	N. J. Chynoweth	204
	G. B. Muston	308 S
	G. F. Parker	204
	D. W. B. Robinson	305

Episcopal Church of Brazil

Central Brazil	A. G. Soria	307
Northern Brazil	E. K. Sherrill	202 C
South Central Brazil	S. Takatsu	105
Southern Brazil	A. R. Kratz (Abp)	301

Church of the Province of Burma

Commissary for Burma bishops	Chandu Ray	211

Anglican Church of Canada

Primate	E. W. Scott (Abp)	309
Algoma	F. F. Nock	108 C
The Arctic	J. R. Sperry	107
Athabasca	F. H. W. Crabb (Abp)	203 S; 213
Brandon	J. F. S. Conlin	110
British Columbia	F. R. Gartrell	205 C
Caledonia	D. W. Hambidge	207
Calgary	M. L. Goodman	201
Cariboo	J. S. P. Snowden	205
Central Newfoundland	M. Genge	310
E. Newfoundland and Labrador	R. L. Seaborn (Abp)	307 C
Edmonton	J. A. W. Langstone	308
Fredericton	H. L. Nutter	105
Huron	T. D. B. Ragg	208
Keewatin	H. J. P. Allan	206
Kootenay	R. E. F. Berry	109
Montreal	R. Hollis	302
New Westminster	T. D. Somerville (Abp)	301 C
Niagara	J. C. Bothwell	204 C
Nova Scotia	G. F. Arnold	102
Ontario	H. G. Hill	304
Ottawa	W. J. Robinson	211
Qu'Appelle	M. G. Peers	202
Quebec	A. Goodings	111
Rupert's Land	B. Valentine	209
Saskatchewan	H. V. R. Short	210

Saskatoon	D. A. Ford	209
Toronto	L. S. Garnsworthy	103
Western Newfoundland	S. S. Payne	101
Yukon	J. T. Frame	103
Assistants	E. K. Clarke	308
	A. A. Read	212
	M. C. Robinson	201 S

Church of the Province of Central Africa

Botswana	C. S. Mallory	102
Lusaka	F. Mataka	203
Mashonaland	J. P. Burrough	111
Matabeleland	R. W. S. Mercer	104
Northern Zambia	J. M. Mabula	106
Southern Malawi	D. S. Arden (Abp)	302
Lake Malawi	P. N. Nyanja	211

Church of England

Bath and Wells	J. M. Bickersteth	308
Birmingham	H. W. Montefiore	305
Blackburn	R. A. S. Martineau	201
Bradford	R. S. Hook	209 C
Bristol	E. J. Tinsley	306
Carlisle	H. D. Halsey	206
Chelmsford	A. J. Trillo	305
Chester	H. V. Whitsey	104
Chichester	E. W. Kemp	212
Coventry	J. Gibbs	202
Derby	C. W. J. Bowles	210 C; 213
Durham	J. S. Habgood	111 S
Ely	P. K. Walker	105 S
Exeter	E. A. J. Mercer	302
Gloucester	J. Yates	102
Guildford	D. A. Brown	211 S; 213
Hereford	J. R. G. Eastaugh	203; 213 C
Leicester	R. R. Williams	208
Lichfield	K. J. F. Skelton	310
Lincoln	S. W. Phipps	205
Liverpool	D. S. Sheppard	204 S
London	G. A. Ellison	201 C
Manchester	P. C. Rodger	307
Newcastle, UK	R. O. Bowlby	308
Norwich	M. A. P. Wood	110

Peterborough	D. R. Feaver	304
Portsmouth	A. R. M. Gordon	204
Ripon	D. N. Young	202
Rochester, UK	R. D. Say	309 C
St Albans	R. A. K. Runcie	304 C
St Edmundsbury and Ipswich	L. W. Brown	108
Salisbury	G. E. Reindorp	301
Sheffield	W. G. Fallows	208
Sodor and Man	V. S. Nicholls	103
Southwark	A. M. Stockwood	207
Southwell	J. D. Wakeling	209
Truro	G. D. Leonard	210
Wakefield	C. C. W. James	109
Winchester	J. V. Taylor	106
Worcester	R. W. Woods	101
York	S. Y. Blanch (Abp)	104
Assistants	D. S. Cross	207
	T. R. Hare	107
	J. D. G. Kirkham	309
	M. H. Maddocks	101
	G. J. Paul	303
	S. E. Verney	110

Church of the Province of The Indian Ocean

Antananarivo	E. Randrianovona	305
Diego Suarez	G. Josoa	202
Mauritius	E. U. T. Huddleston (Abp)	111
Seychelles	G. C. Briggs	209
Tamatave	S. Rafanomezana	310

Church of Ireland

Armagh	G. O. Simms (Abp)	108
Cashel and Ossory	J. W. Armstrong	310
Clogher	R. W. Heavener	307 S
Connor	A. H. Butler	109 C
Derry and Raphoe	R. H. A. Eames	105
Down and Dromore	G. A. Quin	110
Dublin	H. R. McAdoo (Abp)	305 C
Kilmore	E. F. B. Moore	111
Limerick and Killaloe	E. Owen	212
Meath and Kildare	D. A. R. Caird	201
Tuam	J. C. Duggan	102 S

Japan Holy Catholic Church		
Hokkaido	J. M. Watanabe	201
Kobe	T. Y. Nakamichi	306
North Kanto	P. S. Saito	210
Okinawa	P. S. Nakamura	202
Osaka	C. I. Kikawada	106
Tohoku	S. M. Imai (Senior Bishop, representing the Primate)	305
Episcopal Church in Jerusalem and the Middle East		
Cyprus and the Gulf	L. J. Ashton	208; 213
Egypt	I. Musaad	102
Iran	H. B. Dehqani-Tafti (Pres. Bp)	205
Jerusalem	F. I. Haddad	211
Assistant	A. K. Cragg	304
Church of the Province of Kenya		
Maseno North	J. I. Mundia	305
Maseno South	J. H. Okullu	103 S
Mombasa	P. Mwang'ombe	104
Mount Kenya East	D. M. Gitari	203
Mount Kenya South	S. Magua	301
Nairobi	F. H. Olang' (Abp)	101
Nakuru	M. Kuria	302
Assistant	C.Nzano	308
Church of the Province of Melanesia		
Central Melanesia	N. K. Palmer (Abp)	103
Malaita	L. Alufurai	105
New Hebrides	D. A. Rawcliffe	305
Ysabel	D. Tuti	308
Church of the Province of New Zealand		
Aotearoa	M. A. Bennett	102
Auckland	E. A. Gowing	210
Christchurch	W. A. Pyatt	106
Dunedin	P. W. Mann	107
Nelson	P. E. Sutton	305
Polynesia	J. L. Bryce	201; 213
Waiapu	P. A. Reeves	207 S
Waikato	A. H. Johnston (Abp)	309
Wellington	E. K. Norman	206

Anglican Church of Papua New Guinea

Aipo Rongo	J. C. Ashton	303
Dogura	R. E. Sanana	208
New Guinea Islands	B. C. Meredith	301
Popondota	G. Ambo	205
Port Moresby	G. D. Hand (Abp)	106

Episcopal Church in Scotland

Aberdeen and Orkney	F. C. Darwent	102
Argyll and the Isles	G. K. B. Henderson	104
Brechin	L. E. Luscombe	111
Edinburgh	A. I. M. Haggart (Primus)	106
Glasgow	F. Goldie	304 S
Moray, Ross, and Caithness	G. M. Sessford	109
St Andrews	M. G. Hare Duke	302

Church of the Province of South Africa

Bloemfontein	F. A. Amoore	304
Cape Town	B. B. Burnett (Abp)	306
Damaraland	C. O. Winter	105
George	W. J. Manning	301
Grahamstown	K. C. Oram	212 C
Johannesburg	T. J. Bavin	305 S
Kimberley and Kuruman	G. C. Chadwick	107 S
Lesotho	P. S. Mokuku	104
Lebombo	D. S. Sengulane	105
Natal	P. W. R. Russell	208 C
Port Elizabeth	B. R. Evans	310
Pretoria	M. Nuttall	206
St Helena	G. K. Giggall	110
St John's	J. L. Schuster	205
Swaziland	B. N. Mkhabela	309
Zululand	L. B. Zulu	103
Assistants	J. Kauluma	111
	P. J. Litumbe	202
	P. M. Matolengwe	201
	M. S. Ndwandwe	108
	G. A. Swartz	109 S
	D. M. Tutu	101

Anglican Council for South America

Argentina	R. S. Cutts	207
Northern Argentina	P. B. Harris	212

Paraguay	D. Milmine	206 S
Peru	D. R. J. Evans	206
Assistant	I. A. Morrison	302

Province of the Episcopal Church of the Sudan

Juba	E. J. Ngalamu (Abp)	211
Omdurman	B. T. Shukai	205
Rumbek	B. W. Yugusuk	206
Yambio	Y. K. Dotiro	306

Church of the Province of Tanzania

Central Tanganyika	Y. Madinda	203 C
Dar-es-Salaam	J. Sepeku (Abp)	306
Masasi	G. H. Chisonga	308
Morogoro	G. Chitemo	107
Ruvuma	M. D. L. Ngahyoma	104
Southwest Tanganyika	J. W. Mlele	109
Victoria Nyanza	J. O. Rusibamayila	303
Western Tanganyika	M. Kahurananga	108
Zanzibar and Tanga	Y. Jumaa	105
Assistant	A. F. Mohamed	207

Church of the Province of Uganda, Rwanda, Burundi, and Boga-Zaire

Boga-Zaire	P. B. Ridsdale	303
Bujumbura	S. Sindamuka	206
Bukavu	B. Ndahura	306
Bukedi	Y. Okoth	307
Bunyoro-Kitara	Y. K. Ruhindi	209
Busoga	C. K. Bamwoze	205
Butare	J. Ndandali	308
East Ankole	Amos Betungura	302
Kampala	S. G. Wani (Abp)	202
Karamoja	W. B. Herd	109
Kigali	A. Sebununguri	204
Kigezi	F. Kivengere	107
Lango	M. Otim	107
Madi and West Nile	R. U. Ringtho	310
Mbale	J. Wasikye	109
Mityana	Y. B. Mukasa	211
Namirembe	D. K. Nsubuga	201
Northern Uganda	B. Y. Ogwal	301
Ruwenzori	Y. K. Rwakaikara	110

Soroti	G. Ilukor	103
West Ankole	Y. K. Bamunoba	304
West Buganda	D. C. Senyonjo	306
Assistants	A. L. Gonahasa	303
	M. Kauma	108 S
	W. Rukirande	208

Episcopal Church in the United States of America

Presiding Bishop	J. M. Allin	110
Alabama	F. C. Stough	310 C
Alaska	D. R. Cochran	106; 213
Albany	W. E. Hogg	102
Arizona	J. M. Harte	212
Arkansas	C. Keller	308
Atlanta	B. J. Sims	308
Bethlehem	L. E. Gressle	105
Central Florida	W. H. Folwell	210
Central Gulf Coast	G. M. Murray	109
Central New York	N. Cole	201
Central Pennsylvania	D. T. Stevenson	206
Central Philippines	M. C. Lumpias	303
Chicago	J. W. Montgomery	305
Colorado	W. C. Frey	105
Dallas	A. D. Davies	307
Delaware	W. H. Clark	303
East Carolina	H. A. Elebash	110 C
Eastern Oregon	W. B. Spofford	111
Easton	W. M. Moore	208
Eau Claire	S. H. Atkins	203
Erie	D. J. Davis	101 S
Florida	F. S. Červeny	207
Fond du Lac	W. H. Brady	103 C
Georgia	G. P. Reeves	301
Haiti	L. A. J. Garnier	208
Hawaii	E. L. Browning	109
Idaho	H. L. King	305
Indianapolis	E. W. Jones	209
Kansas	E. C. Turner	207
Kentucky	D. B. Reed	303
Lexington	A. Hosea	209
Liberia	G. D. Browne	207 C
Long Island	R. C. Witcher	205
Los Angeles	R. C. Rusack	210

		PARTICIPANTS
Louisiana	J. B. Brown	204
Maine	F. B. Wolf	309
Maryland	D. K. Leighton	307
Massachusetts	J. B. Coburn	206 C
Michigan	H. C. McGehee	306
Milwaukee	C. T. Gaskell	103
Minnesota	R. M. Anderson	204
Mississippi	D. M. Gray	205
Missouri	W. A. Jones	103
Montana	J. E. Gilliam	306
Nebraska	J. D. Warner	211
Nevada	W. Frensdorff	308 C
New Hampshire	P. A. Smith	207
New Jersey	A. W. Van Duzer	204
New York	P. Moore	106 C
Newark	J. S. Spong	111
North Carolina	T. A. Fraser	209
Northern California	C. R. Haden	201
Northern Indiana	W. C. R. Sheridan	101
Northern Michigan	W. A. Dimmick	212
Northern Philippines	R. A. Abellon	111
North West Texas	W. R. Henton	208
Ohio	J. H. Burt	107 C
Oklahoma	G. N. McAllister	302
Olympia	R. H. Cochrane	101
Oregon	M. P. Bigliardi	108
Pennsylvania	L. C. Ogilby	109
Pittsburgh	R. B. Appleyard	304
Quincy	D. J. Parsons	202
Rhode Island	F. H. Belden	111
Rio Grande	R. M. Trelease	302
Rochester, NY	R. R. Spears	108
San Diego	R. M. Wolterstorff	108
San Joaquin	V. M. Rivera	306 S
South Carolina	G. Temple	203; 213
South Dakota	W. H. Jones	106
South East Florida	J. L. Duncan	201
Southern Ohio	J. M. Krumm	304
Southern Philippines	C. B. Manguramas	203
Southern Virginia	C. C. Vaché	208
South West Florida	E. P. Haynes	202
South Western Virginia	W. H. Marmion	212 S
Springfield	A. W. Hillestad	109

Taiwan	J. Pong	211 C
Tennessee	W. E. Sanders	202
Texas	J. M. Richardson	104
Utah	O. Charles	104
Vermont	R. S. Kerr	203; 213
Virgin Islands	E. M. Turner	101
Virginia	R. B. Hall	106
Washington	J. T. Walker	102 C
West Missouri	A. A. Vogel	107
West Texas	S. F. Bailey	309
West Virginia	R. P. Atkinson	205
Western Kansas	W. Davidson	102
Western Massachusetts	A. D. Stewart	310
Western Michigan	C. E. Bennison	211
Western New York	H. B. Robinson	307
Western North Carolina	W. G. Weinhauer	107
Wyoming	B. G. Jones	309
Province IX		
Dominican Republic	T. A. Isaac	108
Ecuador	A. D. Caceres	106
Guatemala	A. Carral	303
Honduras	H. L. Pina-Lopez	107
Nicaragua	G. E. Haynsworth	207
Northern Mexico	L. R. Romero	204
Panama Canal Zone	L. B. Shirley	309
Puerto Rico	F. Reus-Froylan	104 C
Western Mexico	M. Saucedo	209
Assistants	H. I. Mayson	105
	D. E. Richards	206
	M. L. Wood	310
	J. T. Heistand	301

Church in Wales

Bangor	G. O. Williams (Abp)	303
Llandaff	J. R. W. Poole Hughes	301 S
Monmouth	D. G. Childs	304
St Asaph	H. J. Charles	203; 213
St Davids	E. M. Roberts	101
Swansea and Brecon	B. N. Y. Vaughan	205 S

Church of the Province of West Africa

Aba	H. A. I. Afonya	310

Accra	I. S. M. Lemaire	208
Asaba	R. N. C. Nwosu	111
Benin	J. W. I. Idahosa	101
Egba-Egbado	J. S. Adeniyi	211
Ekiti	J. A. Adetiloye	210
Enugu	G. N. Otubelu	106 S
Gambia and the Rio Pongas	J. R. Elisée	111
Ibadan	T. O. Olufosoye	104
Ijebu	I. B. O. Akintemi	204
Ilesha	J. A. I. Falope	110
Kumasi	J. B. Arthur	212
Kwara	H. Haruna	201
Lagos	F. O. Segun	103
The Niger	J. A. Onyemelukwe	208
The Niger Delta	Y. A. Fubara	204
Northern Nigeria	T. E. Ogbonyomi	102
Ondo	E. O. Idowu	210
Owerri	B. C. Nwankiti	302 S
Sierra Leone	M. N. C. O. Scott (Abp)	211
	T. I. Akintayo	108

Church of the Province of the West Indies

Antigua	O. U. Lindsay	106
Barbados	D. W. Gomez	301
Belize	E. A. Sylvester	307
Guyana	A. J. Knight (Abp)	209
Jamaica	H. D. Edmondson	210
Nassau and the Bahamas	M. H. Eldon	309 S
Trinidad and Tobago	C. O. Abdulah	303 S
Venezuela	H. H. Jones	110
Windward Islands	G. C. M. Woodroffe	306 C
Assistants	N. W. de Souza	102
	R. O. George	206
	W. A. Murray	110 S

Extra Provincial

Bermuda	R. A. M. Genders	212
Busan	W. C. H. Choi	306
Colombo	S. W. Fernando	207
Cuba	J. A. Gonzalez	103
Gibraltar	J. R. Satterthwaite	304
Hong Kong	G. H. Baker	302 C
Kuching	B. Temengong	310

Sabah	L. H. S. Chhoa	206
Seoul	P. C. H. Lee	205
Singapore	B. I. Chiu	209
Taejon	M. D. H. Pae	203
West Malaysia	J. G. Savarimuthu	212

Participants from the Anglican Consultative Council

Episcopal members of the Anglican Consultative Council at the Conference have been included within the foregoing list of bishops. The following clerical and lay members of the ACC were also appointed as participants and were present at the Conference:

Mr J. Bikangaga	Uganda	307
Mr J. C. Cottrell	New Zealand	302
Mr J. G. Denton	Australia	310 S
The Ven. S. Kafity	Jerusalem and the Middle East	308
Dr Marion Kelleran (Chairman)	U.S.A.	301
The Rev. E. K. Mosothoane	South Africa	202 S
The Rev. R. T. Nishimura	Japan	309
Mr J. F. M. Smallwood	England	303

Consultants

The Very Rev. J. R. Arnold	England
The Ven. E. G. Buckle	New Zealand
The Very Rev. H. Chadwick	England
The Rev. F. D. Chaplin	Anglican Consultative Council
Dr J. Coleman	Canada
Canon A. O. Dyson	England
Dr B. P. Hall	U.S.A.
The Rt Rev. R. P. C. Hanson	England
The Rev. J. Hartin	Ireland
Canon D. E. Jenkins	England
Mr L. E. M. Kombe	Zambia
Canon Professor J. Macquarrie	England
Canon H. Melinsky	England
Dr Lucy Oommen	North India
Dr J. S. Pobee	Ghana
The Rt Rev. J. A. T. Robinson	England
The Rev. Dr H. R. Smythe	Rome
The Rev. Dr J. R. W. Stott	England

Canon Professor S. W. Sykes	England
Dr Cynthia Wedel	U.S.A.

Consultants were free to range over as many groups and sections as requested their help or in which they had particular interest or expertise.

Observers from other Churches

Baptist World Alliance	The Rev. Dr D. S. Russell
Church of Bangladesh	The Rt Rev. B. D. Mondal
Church of North India	The Rt Rev. R. S. Bhandare
Church of Pakistan	The Rt Rev. Arne Rudvin
Church of South India	The Most Rev. N. D. Ananda Rao Samuel
	The Rt Rev. Solomon Doraisawmy
Disciples of Christ	Dr David M. Thompson
Lusitanian Church	The Rt Rev. Dr L. G. R. Pereira
Lutheran World Federation	The Rev. Dr C. H. Mau
	The Rev. G. Gassman
	The Rev. Dr D. Martensen
	The Rt Rev. A. Aarflot
Mar Thoma Syrian Church	The Most Rev. Dr Alexander Mar Thoma
Old Catholic Church	The Most Rev. M. Kok
	The Rt Rev. G. A. van Kleef
	The Rt Rev. J. Brinkhues
Oriental Orthodox Churches	The Rt Rev. N. Bozobalian
Orthodox Churches	The Most Rev. Athenagoras
	The Very Rev. V. M. Borovoy
Philippine Independent Church	The Rt Rev. Porfirio de la Cruz
	The Rt Rev. D. A. Vilches
Roman Catholic Church	The Rt Rev. Mgr W. A. Purdy
	The Very Rev. Canon R. I. Stewart
	The Rt Rev. C. B. Daly
Spanish Reformed Church	The Rt Rev. R. Taibo
World Alliance of Reformed Churches	The Rev. Dr R. S. Louden
	The Rev. Dr J. Huxtable
World Confessional Families	Dr B. B. Beach
World Council of Churches	The Rev. D. Gill
	The Rev. K. Raiser
World Methodist Council	The Rev. Dr K. Greet

Sections and groups

Section 1: What is the Church for?

Chairman—Bishop Desmond Tutu
Vice-chairman—Archbishop George Simms
Secretary—Canon J. S. Kingsnorth

Groups

101 Christian ethics in today's world
102 Ethics and the individual's changing experience of life
Ethics and secularism
103 Christianity and politics
104 Socialism and Marxism
105 Christian understanding of 'community', and the individual
106 Culture and the twentieth century
The universal Church
107 The Holy Spirit and the Church today
108 Human dignity and freedom
109 Mission
110 Sexuality
Family
111 Twentieth century technology and its relation to human life

Section 2: The people of God and ministry

Chairman—Bishop Douglas Hambidge
Vice-chairman—Archbishop Moses Scott
Secretary—Fr Austin Masters

Groups

201 Authority, universal and local Synodical government
202 Evangelization and mission
203 Ministry, particularly in a rural environment
204 Ministry, particularly in an urban environment
205 The bishop's function within the Church
206 Training for ministry: bishops
Bishops and personal life

207 Training for ministry—of all kinds
208 Lay people and ministry
209 Self-supporting ministry
210 Women and ministry
Ordination of women to the priesthood
211 Other faiths and religions
212 Worship
Liturgical revision
213 Lay presidency of the Eucharist
(This group was added to the Section during the Conference)

Section 3: The Anglican Communion in the world-wide Church[1]

Chairman—Bishop Patrick Rodger
Vice-Chairman—Archbishop Allen Johnston
Secretary—Archdeacon E. S. Light

301 Authority and independence in the Anglican Communion
302 Communication and the Incarnation
Communication in the Anglican Communion
303 Ecumenism: the Anglican Communion; the parish; the World Council of Churches
304 Ecumenism: the Anglican Communion and the Orthodox Churches
The 'Agreed Statement' (Moscow Statement, 1977)
305 Ecumenism: the Anglican Communion and the Roman Catholic Church
The 'Agreed Statements' on Eucharistic Doctrine, Ministry and Ordination, and Authority in the Church
306 Evangelization
Ecumenism and the Kingdom of Christ
307 The Holy Spirit and the Church today
308 Mission; and 'Partners in Mission'
309 Structures in the Anglican Communion
Relating together the Anglican Consultative Council and Lambeth Conference
310 The Gospel and the use of resources
Stewardship
Finance

[1] Original title, 'The role of the Anglican Church among the Churches'.

Hearings

Four of the afternoon sessions of the Conference were given over to plenary Hearings. These were not debates, but opportunities for information to be passed on, or for bishops to make their points of view known to the whole Conference on subjects which were not necessarily those assigned to the particular group or section to which they belonged. Each Hearing began with one or more presentations by invited bishops or consultants, after which (except at the fourth Hearing) contributions were made from the floor. There was no summing-up, nor were any resolutions put or votes taken. The sections and groups were invited to take note of what had been said in Hearings when preparing their reports or proposing resolutions to the Conference.

Hearing A (28th July) Training for ministry in the Church

Chairman: Archbishop Alan Knight (West Indies)

The introductory speeches were made by Bishops Gresford Chitemo of Morogoro, Tanzania (training and training needs in East Africa), Patrick Harris of Northern Argentina (Theological Education by Extension in South America) and David Richards, Director of the Office of Pastoral Development in the Episcopal Church in the U.S.A. (training for episcopal ministry). Most of the contributions to this Hearing, in which the preponderant number of speeches were from the bishops of the Third World, were either on the need for new bishops to be trained for their role or on the shortage of academically excellent and spiritually mature teachers to train people for the ministry in the theological seminaries of the Third World and to relate theological education to the local cultural context.

Hearing B (31st July) Ordination of women to the priesthood

Chairman: Archbishop Gwilym Williams (Wales)

Canon John Macquarrie, Lady Margaret's Professor of Divinity at Oxford University, introduced this Hearing. An abbreviated version of his remarks is printed on pages 116–119 below. In the two hours which followed, there was time to call only 22 out of over 50 bishops who had put down their names to speak. Those who did, were almost equally divided between bishops from

Provinces which ordained women and those who did not. One consultant spoke, as did observers from the Roman Catholic, Old Catholic, and Orthodox Churches, the Church of South India, and the World Methodist Council. The arguments for and against were little rehearsed; the stress of the Hearing fell on sharing information about the experiences of those who had taken this step, and on trying to assess its likely effects on ecumenical dialogue and the unity and *communio in sacris* of dioceses, Provinces, and the Anglican Communion as a whole.

Hearing C (2nd August) Anglican relations with other Churches

Chairman: Archbishop Bill Burnett (South Africa)

There were three speeches of introduction. The Very Reverend Henry Chadwick, Dean of Christ Church Oxford (consultant) spoke on the work and results of the Anglican-Roman Catholic International Commission. Bishop Graham Delbridge of Gippsland, Australia, gave an historical survey of Anglican-Orthodox relationships and indicated the many points where further clarification will be necessary as progress continues. The Primus of Scotland, Bishop Alastair Haggart of Edinburgh, gave a personal view of ecumenical discussion (particularly with the Reformed Church) in a land where Anglicans are non-established and form a very small percentage of the Christian population. In the extended Hearing that followed, information was given on the Anglican Centre in Rome, and observers from the Roman Catholic and Orthodox Churches, the Church of South India, the World Alliance of Reformed Churches, and the Lutheran World Federation spoke on the nature, progress, and prospects of their conversations with Anglicans. Bishop Samuel of the Church of South India appealed for closer links between Lambeth Conferences and the bishops of united Churches with ex-Anglican constituents, hoping that more of their bishops could be invited in future. He also asked that steps should be taken to rescind the ruling (in those Churches where it still applies) that visiting CSI presbyters can only officiate in Anglican churches if they undertake not to do so in churches of other denominations. Dr Cynthia Wedel (consultant) reminded us of the existence of the World Council of Churches and Canon Professor Stephen Sykes (consultant) urged each set of bilateral conversations to be aware of the others. Bishops expressed their anxiety about rocks ahead, but were firm in their determination that, since the disunity of the Churches was the greatest anomaly in Christendom, their attempts to resolve it should continue unabated.

Hearing D (4th August) The Anglican Communion and its future

Chairman: Archbishop Donald Arden (Central Africa)

Bishop Jabez Bryce of Polynesia spoke of the cohesive forces within Anglicanism which helped to bind us together as a Communion. Behind the diversity of our liturgies there still lay the spirit of the Book of Common Prayer; the shift from expatriate to indigenous leadership helped stress the national character of our autonomous member Churches, but the international unity of our Communion was preserved through such world meetings as the Lambeth Conference. Great importance attached to the Partners in Mission consultations as a means of cementing the unity of the Anglican Communion, but he found it frustrating to see that the older Churches still found it very difficult to show the younger ones how to help them. Archbishop Ted Scott of Canada recalled us to the divine Source of our Christian (not only our Anglican) future when he said that the ultimate future of the Anglican Communion depends on whether we can be seen as a credible expression of the faith and hope and love that have been made known to Jesus (see pp. 112f below). It is our business so to live and work that we may know the mind of Christ and do the will of God—and to him be the glory!

On the motion of Presiding Bishop John Allin (representing the regional grouping of North America and the West Indies) the conference decided by a very clear vote on a show of hands to hear no further speakers on this subject in full session but to continue their discussion of it in small groups.

The resolutions of the Conference

1. Today's world

The Conference approves the following statement as expressing some of the concerns of the bishops about today's world in which today's Church must proclaim a total Gospel. It is printed here for study, and action wherever possible, by the member Churches.

We, the bishops of the Anglican Communion gathered from many parts of the world, having experienced a deep unity in the conviction of our faith and in our calling as bishops, wish to share with all people some matters of universal concern.

On earlier occasions we have appealed not only to Anglicans but to all Christian people. Today because we have discovered a new dimension of unity in our intense concern for the future well-being of all mankind in the new era of history which we are now entering we dare to appeal also to governments, world leaders, and people, without distinction, because all countries, however nationalistic in sentiment, are now interdependent. No nation is an island unto itself.

The choices before us are real, and so are the consequences of them. On one hand there are great potentialities for advance in human well-being but there are also real possibilities of catastrophic disaster if present attitudes and the expectations of individuals do not swiftly change and if vital problems of society are not confronted and resolved by governments and through international co-operation.

We draw attention to the following areas where there is need for a change in attitude and practice:

1. We need to see the necessary exchange of commodities in the market place as an area where human values can be affirmed and not ignored; to seek to ensure that those involved are not treated merely as functional units but as being worthy of and able to enter into relations of friendship.
2. We need to challenge the assumptions that 'more is better' and 'having is being' which add fuel to the fire of human greed.
3. We need to stress that the well-being of the whole human family is more important than egoistic self-interest.

4. We need to change the focus on technology and see it not as the master with an insidious fascination of its own but as the servant of the world and its people, beginning with those in need. We must face the threat of science and technology as well as their promise.
5. We need to be diverting our planning and action to the development of a new kind of society. Much time is still spent in overtaking problems. We must direct our efforts to the achievement of a kind of society where the economy is not based on waste, but on stewardship, not on consumerism but on conservation, one concerned not only with work but with the right use of leisure. We may need to contemplate a paradox—an increasing use of appropriate technology, while returning, where possible, to many of the values of pre-industrial society. In some places this can include home industries, the local market, the fishing village, and the small farm.
6. We need to recognize that at present all over the world there tends to be a growing urbanization. Many cities are in crisis due to the growing number of people with little hope of freedom of choice. The gap between the rich and the poor, between the powerful and the powerless, continues to grow.
7. We need to recognize that some earlier evaluations of the place of work in human life are becoming dangerously obsolete. In many societies more goods are produced, but there is less employment. We need to orientate education so as to help people develop new attitudes both to work and leisure.
8. We need to help people in the parts of the world classed as economically underdeveloped not to mirror industrialized societies, but to retain or shape a style of life which affirms both the dignity of the person and the value of close human community.
9. We need to help the developed industrial nations and the people who live in them to face the necessity of a redistribution of wealth and trading opportunities. Such a redistribution could place the major burden on those groups within such societies which are already most vulnerable. We need, therefore, to urge such nations to face the challenge to work for much greater internal justice.
10. We need to recognize that expenditure on armaments in disproportionate to sums spent on such essentials as health and education and constitutes a vast misdirection of limited resources that are badly needed for human welfare, especially for the eradication of poverty. The escalation of weapons systems with their ever-increasing technological complexity diverts attention from the real needs of mankind. We call all people to protest, in whatever ways possible, at the escalation of the commerce in armaments of war and to support with every effort

all international proposals and conferences designed to achieve progressive world disarmament in a way that recognizes the need for power balances. New initiatives are urgently required for mutual coexistence and toleration which are essential if real justice and peace are to be established.

11. The resources of our planet are limited; delicate ecological balances can be disturbed by modern technology, or threatened by the toxic effects of human ingenuity. Ways must be found to stop waste, to re-cycle resources and to monitor and control the manufacture of substances dangerous to life and health. The use of nuclear fuel must be subject to the safe and permanent disposal of its toxic by-products. Alternative sources of energy must be harnessed for use.

Such changes will not be easy to make and will require wise leadership from both secular and religious sources. Creative solutions will require both technical knowledge and moral insights. Decisions will be not only difficult but unpopular.

We recognize and acknowledge with gratitude the many people and agencies who have pioneered in thinking and acting towards the future well-being of the human family. We confess that the Churches to which we belong have shared in attitudes and acquiesced in structures which have been hurtful to the true welfare of the peoples of the world.

We do not pretend to a knowledge of the practical solutions for these problems. But we do affirm that God intends all of us to enjoy this planet and not ruin it; he intends all of us, as his children, to live together peaceably and creatively; to use our skills and knowledge not to destroy but to fulfill human potentialities.

We believe that time is running out. Beneath all the choices lies the ultimate choice of life or death. We join with all men of goodwill in appealing that we shall choose life. We know that tasks and situations which to human view seem hopeless can, with the boundless resources of God's grace, be transformed.

2. A response

The Conference believes that a response to the foregoing statement needs to be made at three levels.

First we appeal to leaders and governments of the world:

1. to participate actively in the establishment of a new economic order aimed at securing fair prices for raw materials, maintaining fair prices for manufactured goods, and reversing the process by which the rich become richer and the poor poorer;
2. to consider seriously all efforts towards a peaceful settlement of international disputes;

3. to persist in the search for ways leading to progressive world disarmament, in particular limiting and reducing the production of, and commerce in, arms;
4. so to limit the development of nuclear energy that they guard against the proliferation of nuclear weapons, at the same time applying every effort to the development of alternative sources of energy;
5. aware that the world is one indivisible system in its operation, to provide that those whose lives are affected by global decisions should be heard in the formulation of policies;
6. to pay attention to human needs in the planning of cities, especially in those places where growing industrialization brings people together in such numbers that human dignity is at risk;
7. to make provision for a new understanding of the place of work in the life of individuals. If the human race as a whole is to reassess its philosophy of economic growth in order to conserve our environment, we will have to find new ways of human fulfilment, paying as much attention to leisure as to paid employment. This needs re-education and a re-distribution of resources at national and international levels.

Second we call on the Churches and in particular the Anglican Communion:

1. to make provision locally to educate their membership into an understanding of these issues;
2. in the face of growing urbanization all over the world to make urgent provision for the training of lay and pastoral leadership in urban mission and to concentrate the use of their personnel and financial resources ecumenically in order to minister to the growing number of urban people with little hope or freedom of choice.

We recommend that greater attention be paid to the work already being done by agencies both within and outside the Churches, that provision be made for communicating their findings in appropriate forms, and that greater use be made of the specialist skills of our lay members to inform the Church's decision-making on social, economic, and technological issues.

Third we call upon members to exercise their rights as citizens of their respective countries:

1. to create a moral climate which enables governments to act for the benefit of the world community rather than sectional interests;
2. in situations where the interests of minorities are in conflict with large-scale development schemes to give consideration to the needs of persons rather than economic advantage;
3. to review their life-style and use of the world's resources so that the service and well-being of the whole human family comes before the enjoyment of over-indulgent forms of affluence.

3. Human rights

The Conference regards the matter of human rights and dignity as of capital and universal importance. We send forth the following message as expressing our convictions in Christ for the human family world-wide.

We deplore and condemn the evils of racism and tribalism, economic exploitation and social injustices, torture, detention without trial and the taking of human lives as contrary to the teaching and example of our Lord in the Gospel. Man is made in the image of God and must not be exploited. In many parts of the world these evils are so rampant that they deter the development of a humane society. Therefore,

1. we call on all governments to uphold human dignity; to defend human rights, including the exercise of freedom of speech, movement, and worship, in accordance with the United Nations Declaration of Human Rights; the right to be housed, freedom to work, the right to eat, the right to be educated; and to give human value and worth precedence over social and ethnic demarcations, regardless of sex, creed, or status;
2. we thank God for those faithful Christians who individually and collectively witness to their faith and convictions in the face of persecution, torture, and martyrdom; and for those who work for and advocate human rights and peace among all peoples; and we assure them of our prayers, as in penitence and hope we long to see the whole Church manifesting in its common life a genuine alternative to the acquisitiveness and division which surround it, and indeed penetrate it;
3. we pledge our support for those organizations and agencies which have taken positive stands on human rights, and those which assist with refugee problems;
4. we urge all Anglicans to seek positive ways of educating themselves about the liberation struggle of peoples in many parts of the world;
5. finally we appeal to all Christians to lend their support to those who struggle for human freedom and who press forward in some places at great personal and corporate risk; we should not abandon them even if the struggle becomes violent. We are reminded that the ministry of the Church is to reveal the love of God by faithful proclamation of his Word, by sacrificial service, and by fervent prayers for his rule on earth.

4. Economic development and minority cultural groups

The Conference believes that a caring Church must be ready to resist and oppose the unheeding advance of economic development where it treats minority cultural groups as disposable.

5. War and violence

1. Affirming again the statement of the Lambeth Conferences of 1930 (resolution 25), 1948, and 1968 that 'war as a method of settling international disputes is incompatible with the teaching and example of Our Lord Jesus Christ', the Conference expresses its deep grief at the great suffering being endured in many parts of the world because of violence and oppression. We further declare that the use of the modern technology of war is the most striking example of corporate sin and the prostitution of God's gifts.

2. We recognize that violence has many faces. There are some countries where the prevailing social order is so brutal, exploiting the poor for the sake of the privileged and trampling on people's human rights, that it must be termed 'violent'. There are others where a social order that appears relatively benevolent nevertheless exacts a high price in human misery from some sections of the population. There is the use of armed force by governments, employed or held in threat against other nations or even against their own citizens. There is the worldwide misdirection of scarce resources to armaments rather than human need. There is the military action of victims of oppression who despair in achieving social justice by any other means. There is the mindless violence that erupts in some countries with what seems to be increasing frequency, to say nothing of organized crime and terrorism, and the resorting to violence as a form of entertainment on films and television.

3. Jesus, through his death and resurrection, has already won the victory over all evil. He made evident that self-giving love, obedience to the way of the Cross, is the way to reconciliation in all relationships and conflicts. Therefore the use of violence is ultimately contradictory to the Gospel. Yet we acknowledge that Christians in the past have differed in their understanding of limits to the rightful use of force in human affairs, and that questions of national relationships and social justice are often complex ones. But in the face of the mounting incidence of violence today and its acceptance as a normal element in human affairs, we condemn the subjection, intimidation, and manipulation of people by the use of violence and the threat of violence and call Christian people everywhere:

   a. to re-examine as a matter of urgency their own attitude towards, and their complicity with, violence in its many forms;

   b. to take with the utmost seriousness the questions which the teaching of Jesus places against violence in human relationships and the use of armed force by those who would follow him, and the example of redemptive love which the Cross holds before all people;

c. to engage themselves in non-violent action for justice and peace and to support others so engaged, recognizing that such action will be controversial and may be personally very costly;

d. to commit themselves to informed, disciplined prayer not only for all victims of violence, especially for those who suffer for their obedience to the Man of the Cross, but also for those who inflict violence on others;

e. to protest in whatever way possible at the escalation of the sale of armaments of war by the producing nations to the developing and dependent nations, and to support with every effort all international proposals and conferences designed to place limitations on, or arrange reductions in, the armaments of war of the nations of the world.

6. Prayer

Since prayer, both corporate and personal, is central to the Christian life, and therefore essential in the renewal of the Church, the fulfilling of the Christian mission, and the search for justice and peace, the Conference gives thanks for all who are endeavouring to increase and strengthen the companionship of prayer throughout the world, and joins in calling the whole Christian community to share personal prayer daily and corporate services of prayer on regular and special occasions.

We also invite all who desire and labour for justice and peace in this world to join with us each day in a moment of prayerful recollection of the needs for a just peace among all people.

7. The Holy Spirit and the Church

1. The Conference rejoices at the abundant evidence from many parts of the world that there is renewed awareness of the power and gifts of God's Holy Spirit to cleanse, sustain, empower, and build up the Body of Christ.
2. We have seen increased instances of parish life being renewed, of individual ministries becoming effective agencies of God's power to heal and reconcile, of witness to the faith and proclamation of the Gospel with converting power, and of a deeper involvement in the sacramental life of the Church.
3. We rejoice at the prompting of God's Spirit within the many expressions of ecumenicity among Christians, for the new forms of Christian communal life springing up and for Christian witness on behalf of world peace and the affirmation of freedom and human dignity.
4. The Conference, therefore, recalls the entire Anglican Communion to a new openness to the power of the Holy Spirit; and offers the following guidance to the Church, in the light of the several ways this Spirit-filled activity may be best understood and represented in the life of the parish.

a. We all should share fully and faithfully in the balanced corporate and sacramental life of the local parish church. Informal services of prayer and praise need this enrichment in the same way as the sacramental life needs the enrichment of informal prayer and praise.

b. We all should ensure that reading and meditation of the Bible be part of the normal life of the parish and be accompanied by appropriate study of scholarly background material so that the Scripture is understood in its proper context. Those who search to understand the scholarly background material in their reading of the Bible should ensure that they do so under the guidance of the Holy Spirit, so that the Scripture is understood in its proper context.

c. We all should search out ways to identify with those who suffer and are poor, and be involved personally in efforts to bring them justice, liberation, healing, and new life in Christ.

d. We should remember always that the power of the Spirit is not to be presented as either an exemption from suffering or a guarantee of success in this life. The road from Palm Sunday to Pentecost must pass through Good Friday and Easter. It is at the Cross that new life through the Holy Spirit is found; and in the shadow of the Cross that Christians must pray 'Come, Holy Spirit'.

8. The Church's ministry of healing

The Conference praises God for the renewal of the ministry of healing within the Churches in recent times and reaffirms:

1. that the healing of the sick in his Name is as much part of the proclamation of the Kingdom as the preaching of the good news of Jesus Christ;
2. that to neglect this aspect of ministry is to diminish our part in Christ's total redemptive activity;
3. that the ministry to the sick should be an essential element in any revision of the liturgy (see the report of the Lambeth Conference of 1958, p. 2.92).

9. Stewardship

1. The Conference calls for continuing emphasis on stewardship teaching and practice. We urge all Anglicans, especially in the western world, to review their value systems, so that life-styles may become related to necessities rather than affluence and consumerism. We commend the biblical principle of tithing as a guide for normal Christian living.
2. In the opinion of the Conference, the scriptural injunction 'he who would be chief among you, let him be the servant of all' requires bishops to reject pretentious life-styles and by example to lead their clergy and

people in the wise use of their personal resources and also those of the Church.

3. We ask that dioceses should increasingly share their financial resources (by a specific amount each year) and skilled persons with those whose resources are more slender.

10. Human relationships and sexuality

The Conference gladly affirms the Christian ideals of faithfulness and chastity both within and outside marriage, and calls Christians everywhere to seek the grace of Christ to live lives of holiness, discipline, and service in the world, and commends to the Church:

1. the need for theological study of sexuality in such a way as to relate sexual relationships to that wholeness of human life which itself derives from God, who is the source of masculinity and femininity;
2. the need for programmes at diocesan level, involving both men and women,

   a. to promote the study and foster the ideals of Christian marriage and family life, and to examine the ways in which those who are unmarried may discover the fullness which God intends for all his children;

   b. to provide ministries of compassionate support to those suffering from brokenness within marriage and family relationships;

   c. to emphasize the sacredness of all human life, the moral issues inherent in clinical abortion, and the possible implications of genetic engineering.
3. While we re-affirm heterosexuality as the Scriptural norm, we recognize the need for deep and dispassionate study of the question of homosexuality, which would take seriously both the teaching of Scripture and the results of scientific and medical research. The Church, recognizing the need for pastoral concern for those who are homosexual, encourages dialogue with them.

   (We note with satisfaction that such studies are now proceeding in some member Churches of the Anglican Communion).

11. Issues concerning the whole Anglican Communion

The Conference advises member Churches not to take action regarding issues which are of concern to the whole Anglican Communion without consultation with a Lambeth Conference or with the episcopate through the Primates Committee, and requests the primates to initiate a study of the nature of authority within the Anglican Communion.

12. Anglican conferences, councils, and meetings

The Conference asks the Archbishop of Canterbury, as President of the Lambeth Conference and President of the Anglican Consultative Council, with all the primates of the Anglican Communion, within one year to initiate consideration of the way to relate together the international conferences, councils, and meetings within the Anglican Communion so that the Anglican Communion may best serve God within the context of the one, holy, catholic, and apostolic Church.

13. Lambeth Conferences

In order that the guardianship of the faith may be exercised as a collegial responsibility of the whole episcopate, the Conference affirms the need for Anglican bishops from every diocese to meet together in the tradition of the Lambeth Conference and recommends that the calling of any future Conference should continue to be the responsibility of the Archbishop of Canterbury, and that he should be requested to make his decision in consultation with the other primates. While recognizing the great value which many set on the link with Canterbury, we believe that a Conference could well be held in some other province.

14. The Wider Episcopal Fellowship

The Conference requests the Archbishop of Canterbury:

1. in consultation with the primates, to convene a meeting of Anglican bishops with bishops of Churches in which Anglicans have united with other Christians, and bishops from those Churches which are in full communion with Anglican Churches; and to discuss with them how bishops from these Churches could best play their part in future Lambeth Conferences;
2. to recognize the deep conviction of this Lambeth Conference that the expressed desire of both the Lusitanian and Spanish Reformed Churches to become fully integrated members of the Anglican Communion should receive both a warm and a positive response.

15. Partners in Mission

The Conference commends the 'Partners in Mission' process to the member Churches of the Anglican Communion and asks them to plan future consultations in accordance with the principles set out in resolution 27 of the second (Dublin, 1973) meeting of the Anglican Consultative Council and resolution 17 of its third (Trinidad, 1976) meeting, and in recommendations 1—8 below:

1. The consultation process is concerned with the meaning of mission as well as its implementation. This point is made clear in the Trinidad report

(page 57, para. 2(b) (ix)), but has not yet been widely received. PIM consultations may be weakened or confused by the failure to recognize that their purpose is to bring about a renewed obedience to mission and not simply to make an existing system efficient. We therefore recommend that each Province seek to educate Anglicans in the meaning of the PIM process and of the significant re-orientation of mission strategy which is involved.

2. One way of achieving this is to encourage the Church to experience the PIM principle at many levels of its life: e.g. between provinces in large national Churches, between dioceses, between a group of parishes, or between parochial and sector ministries.

3. We draw attention to the weakness of the ecumenical dimension in many past consultations and urge the correction of this in the future. Anglicans in any place cannot undertake mission effectively without consulting and planning with fellow-Christians.

4. Churches should not be content with inviting partners only from those areas which share a natural or racial affinity with them. The insights of other cultures, and of various understandings of mission, are vital to growth in a true and balanced theology of mission, and to ensuring the possibility of a creative exchange of resources both personal and material.

5. Representatives of partner Churches do not always have long enough in the host Church and country before the consultation begins. We believe that a period of two weeks, or even longer, would be helpful and appropriate in most situations. Forward planning should allow invitations to be sent out well in advance.

6. We believe the PIM process can help all of us to catch the vision of an interdependent world as well as an interdependent Church. To this end we underline how essential it is that, where possible, the key secular issues should also be well presented in each consultation and by those in society who understand them best.

7. PIM has helped us to develop the concept of sharing rather than of some giving and others receiving. Yet there is an ever-present danger of lapsing into the 'shopping list' way of thinking. At the same time we are sure that consultations should always contain the opportunity for the frank stating of specific needs.

8. Within the Anglican Communion as a whole, thought needs to be given to follow-up as well as co-ordination of response to PIM consultations. We recommend that the ACC gives particular attention to this matter.

16. Sharing resources

The Conference asks the Anglican Consultative Council to assist the member Churches to develop a more effective system for responding to needs identified in Partners in Mission consultations, including the sharing of resources, both of people and of material things.

17. New dioceses

The Conference urges that, when a new diocese is created,

1. adequate financial support should be underwritten by the member Churches concerned, and/or by the Partners in Mission of the new diocese, to ensure against unforeseen financial difficulties;
2. adequate provision should be made for the stipend of the bishop, preferably through the creation of an Episcopal Endowment Fund;
3. when, owing to unforeseen circumstances, a new diocese is faced with financial problems and deficits, it should be aided financially by the member Church concerned and/or by the Partners in Mission of the new diocese;
4. these matters be referred for the consideration of the Anglican Consultative Council at its earliest convenience.

18. Public ministry of the bishop

The Conference affirms that a bishop is called to be one with the apostles in proclaiming Christ's resurrection and interpreting the Gospel, and to testify to Christ's sovereignty as Lord of lords and King of kings. In order to do this effectively, he will give major attention to his public ministry. Reflecting the ministry of the prophets, he will have a concern for the well-being of the whole community (especially of those at a disadvantage) not primarily for the advantage or protection of the Church community. The bishop should be ready to be present in secular situations, to give time to the necessary study, to find skilled advisers and to take sides publicly if necessary (in ecumenical partnership if at all possible) about issues which concern justice, mercy, and truth. Members of the Church should be prepared to see that the bishop is supported in such a ministry.

19. Training for bishops

The Conference asks each member Church to provide training for bishops after election in order more adequately to prepare them for their office; and to provide opportunities for continuing education.

20. Women in the diaconate

The Conference recommends, in accordance with resolution 32 (c) of the Lambeth Conference of 1968, those member Churches which do not at present ordain women as deacons now to consider making the necessary legal and liturgical changes to enable them to do so, instead of admitting them to a separate order of deaconesses.

21. Women in the priesthood

1. The Conference notes that since the last Lambeth Conference in 1968, the diocese of Hong Kong, the Anglican Church of Canada, the Episcopal Church in the United States of America, and the Church of the Province of New Zealand have admitted women to the presbyterate, and that eight other member Churches of the Anglican Communion have now either agreed or approved in principle or stated that there are either no fundamental or no theological objections to the ordination of women to the historic threefold ministry of the Church.

   We also note that other of its member Churches have not yet made a decision on the matter. Others again have clearly stated that they do hold fundamental objections to the ordination of women to the historic threefold ministry of the Church.
2. The Conference acknowledges that both the debate about the ordination of women as well as the ordinations themselves have, in some Churches, caused distress and pain to many on both sides. To heal these and to maintain and strengthen fellowship is a primary pastoral responsibility of all, and especially of the bishops.
3. The Conference also recognizes

   a. the autonomy of each of its member Churches, acknowledging the legal right of each Church to make its own decision about the appropriateness of admitting women to Holy Orders;

   b. that such provincial action in this matter has consequences of the utmost significance for the Anglican Communion as a whole.
4. The Conference affirms its commitment to the preservation of unity within and between all member Churches of the Anglican Communion.
5. The Conference therefore

   a. encourages all member Churches of the Anglican Communion to continue in communion with one another, notwithstanding the admission of women (whether at present or in the future) to the ordained ministry of some member Churches;

   b. in circumstances in which the issue of the ordination of women has caused, or may cause, problems of conscience, urges that every action possible be taken to ensure that all baptized members of the Church continue to be in communion with their bishop and that every opportunity be given for all members to work together in the mission of the Church irrespective of their convictions regarding this issue;

c. requests the Anglican Consultative Council

i. to use its good offices to promote dialogue between those member Churches which ordain women and those which do not, with a view to exploring ways in which the fullest use can be made of women's gifts within the total ministry of the Church in our Communion; and

ii. to maintain, and wherever possible extend, the present dialogue with Churches outside the Anglican family.

6. Consistent with the foregoing, this Conference

a. declares its acceptance of those member Churches which now ordain women, and urges that they respect the convictions of those provinces and dioceses which do not,

b. declares its acceptance of those member Churches which do not ordain women, and urges that they respect the convictions of those provinces and dioceses which do;

c. with regard to women who have been ordained in the Anglican Communion being authorized to exercise their ministry in provinces which have not ordained women, we recommend that, should synodical authority be given to enable them to exercise it, it be exercised only

i. where pastoral need warrants and

ii. where such a ministry is agreeable to the bishop, clergy, and people where the ministry is to be exercised and where it is approved by the legally responsible body of the parish, area, or institution where such a ministry is to be exercised.

7. We recognize that our accepting this variety of doctrine and practice in the Anglican Communion may disappoint the Roman Catholic, Orthodox and Old Catholic Churches, but we wish to make it clear

a. that the holding together of diversity within a unity of faith and worship is part of the Anglican heritage;

b. that those who have taken part in ordinations of women to the priesthood believe that these ordinations have been into the historic ministry of the Church as the Anglican Communion has received it; and

c. that we hope the dialogue between these other Churches and the member Churches of our Communion will continue because we believe that we still have understanding of the truth of God and his will to learn from them as together we all move towards a fuller catholicity and a deeper fellowship in the Holy Spirit.

8. This Conference urges that further discussions about the ordination of women be held within a wider consideration of theological issues of ministry and priesthood.

For the Motion	316
Against	37
Abstentions	17

22. Women in the episcopate

While recognizing that a member Church of the Anglican Communion may wish to consecrate a woman to the episcopate, and accepting that such member Church must act in accordance with its own constitution, the Conference recommends that no decision to consecrate be taken without consultation with the episcopate through the primates and overwhelming support in any member Church and in the diocese concerned, lest the bishop's office should become a cause of disunity instead of a focus of unity.

23. Liturgical information

The Conference welcomes and commends the adoption of a common structure for the Eucharist as an important unifying factor in our Communion and ecumenically. We ask provincial liturgical committees to continue to keep in touch with one another by circulating work in progress to the chairmen of the other liturgical committees through the good offices of the Secretary General of the Anglican Consultative Council.

24. A common lectionary

The Conference recommends a common lectionary for the Eucharist and the Offices as a unifying factor within our Communion and ecumenically; and draws attention to the experience of those Provinces which have adopted the three-year Eucharistic lectionary of the Roman Catholic Church.

25. An Anglican doctrinal commission

The Conference endorses the proposal suggested in resolution 8 of the third (Trinidad, 1976) meeting of the Anglican Consultative Council, to set up an Inter-Anglican Theological and Doctrinal Advisory Commission, and asks the Standing Committee of the ACC to establish the Commission with the advice of the primates, and the primates and Provinces, by whatever means they feel best, to review its work after a period of not more than five years.

26. An association of French-speaking dioceses

The Conference gives thanks to God for the special role and witness of the French-speaking dioceses of our Communion. We learned with deep interest of the emergence of a French-speaking Province in Central Africa. We recognize the special difficulties of French-speaking dioceses in communication, in the production of literature, and in training for the ministry. We call for the active encouragement, under the Partners in

Mission scheme, for all forms of support from the dioceses of our Communion to French-speaking Provinces and dioceses.

27. Service in the world-wide Church

The Conference requests that in order to encourage world-wide service by the clergy and lay servants of the Church, all member Churches be asked to make adequate provision for the future service of those returning to their home Province after a term of duty elsewhere, and also to ensure that ultimate retirement and other relevant provisions and fully protected, either in their home country or in the country of service.

28. Ecumenical relationships

The Conference:

1. re-affirms the readiness of the Anglican Communion as already expressed in resolution 44(c) of the Lambeth Conference of 1968 (with reference to the Uppsala Assembly of the World Council of Churches), to 'work for the time when a genuinely universal council may once more speak for all Christians';
2. acknowledges the pressing need stated by the Nairobi Assembly of the WCC that we should develop more truly sustained and sustaining relationships among the Churches, as we look towards the time when we can enjoy full conciliar fellowship (see *Breaking Barriers: Nairobi 1975*, page 60);
3. encourages the member Churches of the Anglican Communion to pursue with perseverance and hopefulness the search for full communion and mutual recognition of ministries between themselves and other World Confessional Families and the Methodist and Baptist Churches both internationally and locally, on the basis of the Lambeth Quadrilateral and the counsel offered by successive meetings of the Anglican Consultative Council;
4. calls on member Churches of the Anglican Communion to review their commitment to ecumenical structure as well as bilateral conversations at various levels with a view to strengthening the common advance by all Churches to the goal of visible unity;
5. notes that many Christians belong to Churches not members of the World Council of Churches and wishes to develop the opportunities for dialogue and common action with these Churches when appropriate. In particular, the Conference welcomes the participation of Anglican lay persons, priests, and bishops in the Lausanne Congress on World Evangelism of 1974 and subsequent meetings, in which many of these Churches are represented.

29. The World Council of Churches

The Conference urges that, in this thirtieth anniversary year of the World Council of Churches, all Churches of the Anglican Communion re-affirm their support and strengthen their understanding of this body, which is not only the most comprehensive expression of the ecumenical movement, but also the chief vehicle of world-wide ecumenical co-operation and service. It also asks the World Council of Churches to accept the guidance given through Section 3 of the Conference, considering war and violence;

1. to re-examine our complicity with violence in its many forms;
2. to take with the utmost seriousness the question which the teaching of Jesus places against *all* violence in human relationships.

30. Inter-Church relations: definitions of terms

The Conference requests the Anglican Consultative Council, in consultation with other Churches, to formulate appropriate definitions of terms used in inter-Church relations.

31. Relations with Lutheran Churches

The Conference encourages Anglican Churches together with Lutheran Churches in their area:

1. to study the report entitled 'Anglican–Lutheran International Conversations' (the Pullach Report, 1972), resolution 2 of the second meeting (Dublin, 1973) and resolution 5 of the third meeting (Trinidad, 1976) of the Anglican Consultative Council;
2. to give special attention to our ecclesial recognition of the Lutheran Church on the basis of these reports and resolutions; and
3. to seek ways of extending hospitality and of engaging in joint mission.

32. Relations with united Churches

The Conference requests that those member Churches that have placed limitations on the ministry among them of episcopally ordained clergy from united Churches with which they are in communion be asked to reconsider these restrictions so that the same courtesy might be accorded to the clergy of those Churches as to those of other Churches in communion with us.

33. The Anglican–Roman Catholic International Commission

The Conference:

1. welcomes the work of the Anglican–Roman Catholic International Commission which was set up jointly by the Lambeth Conference of 1968 and by the Vatican Secretariat for Promoting Christian Unity;

2. recognizes in the three Agreed Statements of this Commission[1] a solid achievement, one in which we can recognize the faith of our Church, and hopes that they will provide a basis for sacramental sharing between our two Communions if and when the finished Statements are approved by the respective authorities of our Communions;
3. invites ARCIC to provide further explication of the Agreed Statements in consideration of responses received by them;
4. commends to the appropriate authorities in each Communion further consideration of the implications of the Agreed Statements in the light of the report of the Joint Preparatory Commission (the Malta Report received by the Lambeth Conference 1968—see p. 134 of its report), with a view to bringing about a closer sharing between our two Communions in life, worship, and mission;
5. asks the Secretary General of the Anglican Consultative Council to bring this resolution to the attention of the various synods of the Anglican Communion for discussion and action;
6. asks that in any continuing Commission, the Church of the South and the East be adequately represented.

34. Anglican–Roman Catholic marriages

The Conference welcomes the report of the Anglican–Roman Catholic Commission on 'The Theology of Marriage and its Application to Mixed Marriages' (1975).

In particular we record our gratitude for the general agreement on the theology of Christian marriage there outlined, and especially for the affirmation of the 'first order principle'[2], of life-long union (i.e. in the case of a break-down of a marriage). We also welcome the recognition that the differing pastoral practices of our two traditions do in fact recognize and seek to share a common responsibility for those for whom '*no* course *absolutely* consonant with the first order principle of marriage as a life-long union may be available'.

We also endorse the recommendations of the Commission in respect of inter-Church marriages:

1. that, after joint preparation and pastoral care given by both the Anglican and Roman Catholic counsellors concerned, a marriage may validly and lawfully take place before the duly authorized minister of either party, without the necessity of Roman Catholic dispensation;
2. that, as an alternative to an affirmation or promise by the Roman Catholic party in respect of the baptism and upbringing of any children,

[1] Eucharist Doctrine (the Windsor statement, 1971), Ministry and Ordination (Canterbury, 1973), and Authority in the Church (Venice, 1976).

[2] See *Anglican–Roman Catholic Marriages* (London, CIO 1975) p. 21, para. 49.

the Roman Catholic parish priest may give a written assurance to his bishop that he has put the Roman Catholic partner in mind of his or her obligations and that the other spouse knows what these are.

We note that there are some variations in different regions in the provisions of Roman Catholic Directories on inter-Church marriages. We nevertheless warmly welcome the real attempts of many Roman Catholic Episcopal Conferences to be pastorally sensitive to those problems arising out of their regulations, which remain an obstacle to the continued growth of fraternal relations between us. In particular, we note a growing Roman Catholic understanding that a decision as to the baptism and upbringing of any children should be made within the unity of the marriage, in which the Christian conscience of both partners must be respected. We urge that this last development be encouraged.

The problems associated with marriage between members of our two Communions continue to hinder inter-Church relations and progress towards unity. While we recognize that there has been an improved situation in some places as a result of the *Motu Proprio,* the general principles underlying the Roman Catholic position are unacceptable to Anglicans. Equality of conscience as between partners in respect of all aspects of their marriage (and in particular with regard to the baptism and religious upbringing of children) is something to be affirmed both for its own sake and for the sake of an improved relationship between the Churches.

35. Anglican–Orthodox theological dialogue

The Conference:

1. welcomes the achievement of the Anglican–Orthodox Joint Doctrinal Commission as expressed in the Moscow Agreed Statement of 1976, and believes that this goes far to realize the hopes about Anglican–Orthodox dialogue expressed at Lambeth 1968;

2. requests the Anglican–Orthodox Joint Doctrinal Commission to continue to explore the fundamental questions of doctrinal agreement and disagreement in our Churches; and to promote regional groups for theological dialogue which would bring to the Commission not only reactions to their work, but also theological issues arising out of local experience;

3. requests that all member Churches of the Anglican Communion should consider omitting the *Filioque* from the Nicene Creed, and that the Anglican–Orthodox Joint Doctrinal Commission through the Anglican Consultative Council should assist them in presenting the theological issues to their appropriate synodical bodies and should be responsible

for any necessary consultation with other Churches of the Western tradition.

36. Cultural identity

The Conference recognizes with thanksgiving to God the growth of the Church across the world and encourages every particular Church to strengthen its own identity in Christ and its involvement with the community of which it is part, expressing its faith through the traditions and culture of its own society except where they are in conflict with the essentials of the Gospel.

37. Other faiths: Gospel and dialogue

1. Within the Church's trust of the Gospel, we recognize and welcome the obligation to open exchange of thought and experience with people of other faiths. Sensitivity to the work of the Holy Spirit among them means a positive response to their meaning as inwardly lived and understood. It means also a quality of life on our part which expresses the truth and love of God as we have known them in Christ, Lord and Saviour.
2. We realize the lively vocation to theological interpretation, community involvement, social responsibility, and evangelization which is carried by the Churches in areas where Hinduism, Buddhism, Taoism, Confucianism, and Islam are dominant, and asks that the whole Anglican Communion support them by understanding, by prayer, and, where appropriate, by partnership with them.
3. We continue to seek opportunities for dialogue with Judaism.

Section 1
What is the Church for?

Chairman: Bishop Desmond Tutu
Vice-chairman: Archbishop George Simms
Secretary: Canon John Kingsnorth

An editorial collation of views expressed in the course of discussion by the section and in its groups during the Conference. The Conference as a whole is responsible only for the resolutions printed on pp. 33–52 of this volume; see the statement on authority on p. 5 above.

1. Introduction
2. Worship and mission
3. The Church as a sign to the world
4. Some particular issues concerning the Church and society
5. The Holy Spirit and the Church today

(For a list of groups and topics, see p. 28 above; for the members of this section in their various groups, see the final column of the lists on pp. 15–26.)

What is the Church for?

1. Introduction

The Church exists for God—to worship him and to be a sign and agent of his Kingdom. Faithfulness to God through Jesus Christ in the Spirit is the basis of its existence, the inspiration of all it does and strives to become. As God in Jesus commits himself to our humanity, the worship of God through Jesus directs us towards every human search for freedom, fulfilment, and joy; and brings us up against everything that distorts, imprisons, or ignores the lives, needs, and hopes of men, women, and children. Because we worship God in his glory we are called to seek the glory of man.

The calling of the Church is therefore clear—to worship and to witness, to serve and to suffer. Our difficulties do not lie in doubts about this calling or in uncertainties about the truth and the power of what God reveals and offers through Jesus and in the Spirit. Our difficulties have two other sources. On the one hand our own sinfulness often distorts or holds up our responses even to what we know or should do or say or be. On the other hand the complexities and turbulence of our societies and of the world at large often leave us bewildered about what is going on and uncertain about what our responses should be. But we also know that God saves from sin and is with us in the midst of bewilderment. Thus our repeated sins do not deprive us of the opportunities to serve God and our neighbours nor does our frequent bewilderment leave us without indication from God as to how we are to begin to seek his will. For us the very continuing of the Church in worship, in fellowship, and in hope, amidst the realities of sin and bewilderment, is itself a sign and sacrament that there is a God in whom all may realistically trust and to whom all may look for salvation.

It is against this background and in the light of this faith that we wish to share some insights and suggestions that have emerged out of our brief time together in which we have exchanged something of our experiences, our understandings, and our perplexities. We report them knowing that they are but tokens and indications of what the people of God can and will learn as they get on, locally and particularly, with the tasks that challenge them and seize the opportunities that open up to them.

2. Worship and mission

The Church is both 'a holy priesthood' to offer God spiritual sacrifices, and 'God's own people' called to proclaim his wonderful deeds (1 Peter 2. 5–9). Worship and mission are, therefore, the main tasks of the Church, but these

functions are often separated. Some faithful churchmen are diligent in their Sunday worship but have no comparable concern for their Christian responsibility in the world. Others are deeply involved in compassionate service, but impatient with the Church's traditional worship. This polarization between worship and mission is both damaging to the Church's health and a serious departure from God's purpose. We are concerned to see it overcome.

Each has within it an element of the other. There is a sense in which worship *is* mission. To attend a Christian place of worship publicly is to identify oneself as a Christian, which is in many parts of the world a costly testimony. In our eucharistic worship we are not only celebrating the Lord's death and resurrection, but actually proclaiming him as Lord (1 Cor. 11.26). Conversely, there is a sense in which mission *is* worship. For worship is our loving response to God and must be expressed not only in liturgical words but also in practical deeds. Worship and mission also stimulate one another. For to acknowledge God's infinite worth moves us to want others to do the same, while to work and witness in the world redounds to the praise and glory of God. So whenever we assemble as the people of God to worship him, it is not in order to escape from the world, but rather to prepare ourselves to return to it. We gather for worship and scatter for mission.

The word 'mission' denotes 'sentness'. It embraces everything the Church is sent into the world to do. What this is we discover from the mission of Jesus, since he specifically made his mission the model of ours when he said 'As the Father sent me, so I send you' (John 20. 21). He came both preaching and serving. The same balanced combination of words and works, of witness and service, of evangelism and social action, is needed in our Christian mission today.

To proclaim the Word will always remain a primary Christian task. For God has entrusted his Church with good news to share with the world. It is good news of his reign, which broke into the world through Jesus Christ. Those who have received God's free gift of new life in Christ have the constant duty, joy, and privilege of sharing the good news with others. This should be the spontaneous overflow of hearts filled with Christ. Yet there is also need for a thorough training of Church members both in personal evangelism and in the nurture of converts into maturity in Christ. Indeed, one of the chief functions of pastors is to equip God's people for their ministry in the Body of Christ (Eph. 4. 12), taking care not to monopolize it themselves.

God still calls some of his people in every Church and country to be cross-cultural messengers of the Gospel. For there are still millions of people in the world who have never heard of Jesus Christ or who have never had an adequate opportunity to respond to him. So missionaries are still urgently needed and should flow freely from and to all countries. Their responsibility is not to export a culturally-conditioned form of Christianity (Western or any other), but humbly to serve the indigenous Church as it seeks to develop or renew its own authentic form of Christianity within its own local culture.

The mission of the Church is not confined to evangelism, however. Jesus did more than proclaim God's Kingdom; he demonstrated it in his own person and in his works of power and love. All human need, whatever form it took, moved him to compassion. Not only did he feed the hungry and heal the sick, but he risked his reputation by championing those whom society rejected and befriending the friendless. We have no doubt that, like Christ and in his Name, the Church today should take its stand alongside the deprived, the disadvantaged, and the oppressed, in the strong solidarity of love. We also believe that it is a legitimate—even an obligatory—extension of Christ's compassion that Christians involve themselves with others in the quest for better social and economic structures. Unjust structures dehumanize people; that is why Christian compassion demands justice for them. Christians are not as powerless as they often think. In some situations only by prayer, suffering, and the silent exhibition of a better way, but in others by the resistance and denunciation of evil, by fearless witness to truth, righteousness, and freedom, by pressure on public opinion and in other ways, it is possible for Christians to help bring about social change, thus acting as the salt and light which Jesus said his followers should be.

Jesus added, however, that if it is to be effective, the salt must retain its saltness and the light must be allowed to shine (Matt. 5. 13–16). In other words, 'being' precedes 'doing', and before the Church can actively engage in mission, it must itself be renewed for mission. Nothing hinders the mission of the Church, both its evangelistic and its social mission, more than its failure to be what it claims to be, and to practise what it preaches.

If we preach the Incarnation, then we must ourselves live by the principle of the Incarnation, humbling ourselves as Christ humbled himself, serving as he served, renouncing affluence and cultivating a simple life-style, and identifying ourselves with the world in its pain.

If we preach the Cross, then we must ourselves take up the Cross and follow Christ, dying to our own self-centredness in order to live for others, loving, forgiving, and serving our enemies, and overcoming evil with good.

If we preach the Resurrection, then we must ourselves live in its power, experiencing deliverance from the bondage of sin and fear of death, and eagerly expecting the completion of the new creation in Christ.

If we preach the Ascension, then we must ourselves submit to the universal authority of the reigning Christ, longing that every tongue should confess him as Lord and that more and more of human society should come under his rule.

If we preach Pentecost, then we must ourselves demonstrate the power of the Holy Spirit in our own lives, as he forms Christ in us and binds us together in love.

If we preach the Church as a reconciled and reconciling community, then we must set ourselves resolutely against the re-erection of the racial, social, and sexual barriers which Christ abolished (Eph. 2. 11 ff., Gal. 3. 28), and must seek his grace to become the united, accepting, caring, and supportive fellowship which he means us to be.

3. The Church as a sign to the world

If the Church has constantly to strive to be sufficiently broken and sufficiently open to act as a sacrament of the love of God, what sort of a community ought it to be?

The Church needs to be a supportive community. It must be a place of healing and restoration for those who know their need of forgiveness and renewal. It must help to make people whole. It must be a community of repentant sinners, who ought to be able to accept and welcome other sinners, because all belong to it only by the mercy and grace of God.

In practice, though, there are difficulties because the Church also, and rightly, tries to witness to Christian standards, and may resent the dilution of its standards by those who fall too obviously below them. The conflict between this openness to sinners and witness against sin is frequently felt most acutely by the clergy, and especially by bishops. On the one hand they stand for the rigorous claims of the Gospel, while on the other hand they want and need to show pastoral concern for those who have fallen short and sometimes feel themselves personally rejected by the Church. This tension at the heart of the Christian community can be constructive if it is understood and accepted and shared by all.

A Church which aims to heal human brokenness must also inevitably be a suffering community. Its concern may not be confined to its own members, however great their needs. Jesus devoted much of his ministry to those whom the world of his day despised. His Cross is present wherever human beings suffer. The Church feeds on broken bread in the Eucharist, which speaks of the brokenness of human life.

Christians have to ask themselves, therefore, how alert they are to the different kinds of suffering in their midst. In addition to the obvious injustices of material poverty and physical oppression, there are more subtle deprivations and disadvantages. To be labelled 'non-White' is to suffer the indignity of being defined in terms of something one is not, and so one's identity is threatened. To have had a poor education is to be constantly outpaced by those who started life with greater advantages. To feel inferior and unwanted is an additional burden on the suffering of those who can find no work.

A suffering community knows about these things, by being where the suffering is. And this poses questions about the style of Church life, and that of its ministers. A Church which seems to belong to a particular class or section of society is not only failing those whom it seems to ignore, but impoverishing its own life as well. A bishop who seems to belong to another world, whether the world of a secure ecclesiastical in-group, or the world of affluence and privilege, is unable to reach those to whom he has been sent.

This is why deliberate attempts to cross the barriers of race, sex, class, and affluence contribute to the Church's own liberation. For suffering is not an end in itself. The Christian message is one of transformation and joy and liberation. But the joy must be the joy of those who have faced the world's pain and overcome it by love. And the liberation must follow judgement, a judgement in these days ministered not least by the world's poor.

A supportive and suffering community can become a liberated and liberating community only as it is willing to lose its life in the service of God's kingdom of love and justice, and in so doing find its life and identity. This is Christ's way. To want liberation by itself on our own terms and in our own strength has too often proved to be the road to further enslavement.

To sum up: the task of the Church as we see it is to unite all people in the worship of God; to proclaim the good news of salvation through faith in Jesus Christ; to work for justice, peace, and freedom in the world and to pray regularly for the poor and oppressed, as well as for those in authority; to affirm Christian standards in matters of behaviour; and to seek constantly to be radically renewed in truth, holiness, and love, that it may visibly embody the Gospel it proclaims.

4. Some particular issues concerning the Church and society

As we enjoy being the Church and as we struggle to be the Church we share in everything that troubles, excites, and confuses our neighbours, our societies, and the world. Faith and membership of the Church in the middle of all this turbulence and change give us a firm standing ground and many indications of how we should live through it all with purpose and with hope. The comments which follow are directed to just a few of the questions where Christian witness has to be given and where its full significance has to be worked out. A Christian should be ready to face the questions realistically and without fear. We rely on God to help us to contribute appropriate answers once we have followed him into the heart of the conflicts, confusions, and suffering.

A. The diversity of cultures and the questioning of cultures

Culture is the soil in which men and women grow, against which they may rebel and yet out of which they draw their sense of identity and belonging.

Many peoples across the world are crying out in pain and bewilderment because their cultures are being belittled or destroyed. Other peoples are suffering the economic deprivation caused by a dominant technological culture. To them the good news is that in God's eyes their culture, their language, and their soil are infinitely precious and of great dignity. This Gospel is acted out by welcoming the contributions of the various cultures to the life of the Church and to our understanding of Christ. The tongues of Pentecost first celebrated the Christian truth that the Gospel may be spoken in different tongues. Ever since that day the Church at her best has taken on the flesh of the culture in which she finds herself.

But Christ is also the ultimate judge of culture. Cultures cannot be left uncriticized, for the Gospel is universal and therefore is not to be identified with any one particular culture or race. For example, subtle evils, like technology's assurance that it can solve all problems, deny a proper Christian understanding of pain and redemptive suffering. Thus in appreciating a culture the Church can never be completely identified with it.

In proclaiming the Gospel therefore the Church must listen receptively in order to appreciate the underlying values expressed in a particular culture. Furthermore, the Church should be an agent in fostering appreciation of the best of those values. Too often in the past the Church has hastily rejected and hastily destroyed long-standing cultural values and on the other hand too hastily approved and adopted new ones.

Often, when a person is converted to Christ, he feels he has died to his old culture. He feels it is too bound up with the 'old man' he has put off. But slowly as he grows in Christian maturity, he rediscovers its abiding value. The process of formation through all the cultural influences that bear on him, and of transformation as he 'puts on Christ', continues during his whole life.

Cultures themselves, like individuals, need transformation. They are transformed by the life-style of transformed individuals, and by the appreciation and criticism that these individuals bring to bear. The Church then, the fellowship of transformed individuals, is salt in a culture, a leaven of change, the protector and preserver of all that is good—but never a mere mirror.

There are great dangers and many unresolved issues in the Christian transformation of culture. Despite these difficulties our faith demands that a Christian be not removed from his culture in order to be a member of the Church: 'And be not conformed to this world, but be ye transformed by the renewing of your mind, that ye may prove what is that good and acceptable and perfect will of God' (Rom. 12. 2) (see resolutions 4 and 36).

B. Ethics in a changing world

How are Christians to decide what is right in a changing world? Some, bewildered by the rate of change and the pressure of external circumstances, are tempted to believe that 'right' and 'wrong' are no longer the firm categories they were once assumed to be. Others, more conscious of the damaging effects of this uncertainty, cling tenaciously to what they regard as traditional moral absolutes, and see the Church as the last stronghold of stability. Some worry about whether Christian moral leaders are developing genuine Christian insights, or following the fashions of the secular world. Others see the Churches as entrenched in attitudes which can be deeply offensive to liberal-minded people, whether believers or not, and wonder whether the secular world may not sometimes have more to say than Christian tradition.

All this can be very confusing unless it is recognized that throughout its history Christian ethical thinking at its best has constantly had to concern itself with the actual circumstances of human life, and the way in which people actually understand the world in which they have to live. But this does not entail a surrender to every passing fashion. Christ was incarnate in a particular place and at a particular time. In our own day, as we seek 'the mind of Christ', we have to discern this in our own place and in our own time. Christ does not necessarily demand of us the same response as he demanded of our grandparents. But in all our response it is the same unchanging Christ whom we seek, and into whose likeness we strive to grow.

Christ leads his people towards an unknown future, where choices may have to be made which have never been made before. Those who are more concerned with safety and prefer to stay where they are, lose sight of the fact that change itself may be a means of strengthening and enlivening faith in Christ, who calls us not to safety but to salvation. Nevertheless we believe that in today's world the Church should give people moral guidance and direction, and that it has failed to do this in recent years. We believe that the Bible gives a description of God's nature as he has revealed it to us, and that this shows us how to behave in each new situation:

God creates. The people and the resources of the world are made by God and they are good (Genesis 1). We must not destroy or waste them because he cares for them, and so must we.

God judges. He demands that his people do what is right and he punishes those who do not obey him. We must work always for justice and the relief of poverty (Micah 3).

God forgives. He has compassion on those who ask him to forgive their sins against him. We must also forgive those who do wrong to us.

God delivers. Especially through the death of Jesus, he delivers us from the consequences of our sins. He makes us free to serve him. We must work for freedom for all from oppression and injustice (Luke 4).

God reconciles. When the human race had turned away from him he made things right again through Jesus. We must work to overcome hatred and violence and bring peace (2 Cor. 5).

God is truth. We must always speak the truth.

God is life. All life is the gift of God, and we must respect all living things. Human life is especially important because God made man to be like him.

God is love. In our behaviour towards other people we must love them as God does. To love them is to care more for them than we do for ourselves.

We must learn to use the resources which are available to us both within our tradition and within the secular wisdom of the day. The Scriptures are the obvious starting point. There is also a strong, and frequently neglected, tradition of Anglican moral theology, much enriched in recent years by careful interdisciplinary studies of current ethical issues. There is the living mind of the Christian community as Christians try together by prayer and study and waiting on the Spirit of God to come to common agreement. There is conscience, though it needs to be stressed that conscience is only reliable when adequate steps have been taken to inform it. There is also common sense and sensitivity. Injunctions not to hurt others, to think through the consequences of our actions and to fulfil the responsibilities given to us, to obey the civil law, and to take care for the stability of society, are among the moral obligations which Christians share with everyone else. But these injunctions cannot be absolute. 'We must obey God rather than men', and there are Christians in our Churches today who know the heavy cost of such obedience.

A further complication is that moral actions, particularly within a body which claims to be a moral guide, have a public dimension to them, and are judged by a watching world. Actions speak louder than words, and a Church which takes a firm moral line on some contemporary issue such as divorce, may have reasoned out the matter with impeccable clarity, yet convey the impression that Christians lack compassion.

Conflicts between the Church's witness and its inner integrity are sometimes unavoidable and it is as well to be aware of them. The mass media intensify the problem, and by their tendency to over-simplify, tempt many to exaggeration and over-confidence. The pressure group shouting out its certainties, and intent on securing publicity by fair means or foul, has achieved new significance in an era of mass communication. Churches are not immune from these temptations, especially when they feel threatened or irrelevant.

Christian moral reflection must always include a real sense of our own fallibility. In seeking Christian discernment we wait in trust on God, who meets us in our weakness, reveals to us his nature and his will, forgives us our sinfulness, and shows us his glory in the face of Jesus Christ.

C. The family

We reaffirm the enduring value and importance of the Christian family. We do so because we are aware that the rapidly-changing patterns of our world are placing enormous strain on that basic unit of our society. Before speaking to some of those pressures we wish to state clearly some ideals for the Christian family which we believe God sets before his Church and which his Church is called to set before the world.

1. Marriage is sacred. It was instituted by God and blessed by our Lord Jesus Christ.
2. Marriage at its deepest and best is a joyful and challenging union issuing in a sense of mutual fulfillment of both husband and wife. Such a relationship requires faithfulness in each partner until the couple is parted by death—for marriage, says the Epistle to the Ephesians, is meant to parallel the ideal relationship of Christ and his Church. Such a commitment requires a self-discipline which issues in a life-giving and lasting love.
3. The gifts bestowed by God upon marriage include full bodily union. We believe that God intends both husband and wife to enjoy their sexual relationship, to delight in their social caring for each other, and to accept the responsibility of parenthood when it stems from such a union. No greater privilege can come to human beings than to share with God in the creation of new life inside the union of a loving marriage.
4. Marriage and the family need the resources of the Christian faith if they are to approach Christian ideals. We commend to Christian families a deeper and fuller participation in the life of the Church. We believe that marriages are deepened by regular prayer, Bible reading and corporate sacramental worship. We urge our clergy to recognize the importance of careful and significant preparation for all aspects of marriage so that these resources of the Spirit might be available to each new married couple. We call upon parents to recognize that they bear the primary responsibility for the growth and nurture of their children in the Christian life and faith. It is parental guidance, compassion, forgiveness, and love that transform even failures into opportunities of growth. Those qualities inevitably reach beyond the family and are instruments of healing in our broken world.

We are not unaware that many today question the future of the family as a social unit. We are alarmed by the accelerating divorce rate especially in the western industrialized nations. We see many aspects of the western single-unit family that are sources of distress. Modern society places enormous emotional demands on a unit which is proving to be too small adequately to meet those demands. The western industrial nations have developed a highly mobile society that has separated generations, and blood relations, and in many cases produced much loneliness and a sense of alienation. The African concept of the extended family is not today paralleled in modern western life. In many modern families in the west grandparents, aunts, uncles, cousins, grandchildren are not significant people, because they live too far away.

It is not sufficient to call for the creation of larger family units for we cannot reverse by our pronouncement the social, economic, and technological forces which have produced the western mobile small family pattern, but we can bear witness to some of the richness that the larger family provided in the past and to the emotional needs in all of us to be members of a larger loving and redeeming community or family.

We urge a rethinking of that peculiarly western tradition which seems to isolate the elderly in separate communities. We believe that the senior generation has many gifts to give the whole society. We would encourage experiments in community living where the basic sacredness of the individual marriage is still upheld. We would urge congregations in urban or rapidly changing neighbourhoods to see a significant part of their ministry in terms of building a larger sense of family to which individual units might readily belong and by which they might be deeply fed.

We recognize that the small family of parents and their children has in many instances produced sensitive and mature people. But experience shows that the potential for destruction also exists in such a small family. Death, physical or mental sickness, or irresponsible behaviour by one member can literally destroy the family and those in it. Modern social and economic conditions also strain this small family unit.

The Church has an urgent task of finding ways to strengthen and support family life, and of helping those who have been victimized by the failure of family life to support them, whether through internal collapse or the pressure of the social system.

We deplore the particular economic policies of certain governments which force long separations of married persons in migratory work camps and mining communities. We deplore the dislocation and abnormal stresses on both the basic humanity and the moral values of the victims of these unjust labour systems.

D. Sexuality—masculinity and femininity

The Lambeth Conference of 1958 recorded, in resolution 112, its profound conviction that the idea of the human family is rooted in the Godhead and that 'all problems of sex relations . . . must be related, consciously and directly, to the creative, redemptive, and sanctifying power of God'.

God is not masculine. Neither is God feminine. God is the source of masculinity and femininity, and of all those human characteristics which are variously called masculine and feminine in different cultures. God's nature is reflected in the balance and interaction between them.

We, in time and space, are sexual creatures. God created us male and female. The wholeness of God can be most directly expressed in the give and take of love between a man and a woman. But this wholeness of God is also present in each individual person, whose total sexuality is expressed through the interplay of masculine and feminine qualities.

The Christian life holds in balance the masculine and the feminine qualities. God's wholeness sets us free. He calls us into mature relationships of inter-dependence with each other—to forgive as we are forgiven, to love as we are loved—our fragmented sexuality transformed by his wholeness.

We commend the study of this theme to the Church, as offering a true basis for all sexual relationships (see resolution 10 (1)).

E. Homosexuality

Today we do not expect everyone to conform to a norm—a sort of average humanness—but rather to rejoice in variety; so the status and rights of homosexuals are being reconsidered.

Homosexuality has rarely received understanding either in Church or in society. Despite much research there is still considerable disagreement about its nature and causes. It is commonly referred to as a deviation, yet many homosexuals do not believe they are abnormal. They do not ask for sympathy, but for recognition of the fact that their homosexual relationship can express mutual love as appropriately for the persons concerned as a heterosexual relationship might for others. The majority of Christians would not willingly agree with this attitude. We assert however that an adequate understanding of, and response to, homosexuality will not be found until society as a whole and Christians in particular, can approach the subject compassionately and without prejudice.

Questions relating to homosexuality are admittedly complex, and we note that these questions are currently the subject of serious study in some parts of the Anglican Communion. There are other places (e.g. in the Church of Africa) where homosexual behaviour has not emerged as a problem. This fact indicates the need for further study as to the possible relationship between homosexuality and environment. There is also particular need for further study of the Scriptural evidence such as Romans 1.18–32 which depicts homosexual behaviour as one of the manifestations of the fragmentation of life in a fallen world.

It is the responsibility of every local Church to become such a warm-hearted, Christ-centred, eucharistic fellowship, that people of every temperament and tendency might find their true unity and fellowship within the total family of Christ, where all are sinners, but all can find the grace and forgiveness of Christ in 'his accepting community' (see resolution 10 (3)).

F. Technology and human life

Technology increases human potentiality for good and evil. It creates unprecedented opportunities and poses unprecedented problems. These are not the kind of problems which can be solved once for all, but they form the constant background of much twentieth-century life. The way they are understood and evaluated depends greatly on the degree of technological development already enjoyed. There are those for whom even piped water and an electricity supply are a distant dream. And there are others who feel themselves trapped in a greedy and extravagant consumer society, which is as wasteful of human skills as it is of natural resources. Some look with longing at the simplicities they have lost, yet few are actually prepared to pay the cost of a return to simplicity. Others have still to assess the true social costs of development.

No single set of policies can cater for such different needs and perceptions. Yet we all live in one world, sharing the same environment, competing for the same limited resources, dependent on one another economically and politically, and increasingly made aware of one another by rapid travel and communications. The issues which have to be faced by different groups and peoples thus form an interlocking whole. Hence while different policies may be appropriate in different settings, a realization of the complexity of the whole is essential for a constructive approach to any part. The immensely widespread ramifications of the energy problem typify all the rest.

Technical advance widens the scope of personal choice; it brings freedom, and this is one of its main attractions. But it can also enslave. The many unforeseen consequences of the motor car are a prime example. Medical advances likewise can increase freedom, but they also multiply the dilemmas of those who have to use them. Test-tube babies may give new hope to infertile women, but at the same time may open the way to further and more dubious possibilities of genetic manipulation. Contraceptive devices are giving a fresh dimension of choice to parents and at the same time are working a revolution in sexual behaviour. The 'green revolution' multiplied food production, and threw out of work those who most needed money to buy the food.

What all these and many other practical issues have in common is their relationship to a total way of life in which the exploitation of new technological possibilities sets the pace. But how long can it go on doing this? What limits of growth are set by the limitations of the earth's natural resources? Can all eventually expect to enjoy the standard of living which some now take for granted? How can human beings start to exercise a wise stewardship of God's world? These are some of the most momentous questions facing humanity.

And over the whole scene hangs a mushroom cloud. War and the threat of war have too often been the motivating force behind technical ingenuity. The results are seen today in the monstrous waste of the armaments race, which threatens human values as much by its diversion of resources and energies as by its unimaginable power of destruction. Only in a peaceful world, where people have learnt to trust one another, can the main efforts of technologists be directed to worthwhile ends.

Those in power are tempted to avoid major problems about world development, and major policy decisions about the kind of world that technology is creating. Sometimes power is used immorally to bring about technical change without consulting the interests of those most involved. It is usual for particular decisions on technical matters to be taken in isolation from one another, so that their general drift is never appreciated or criticized.

It is, therefore, essential for those who are aware of the issues to go on drawing attention to them. Peoples and nations have to be made more sensitive to one another's needs. Anyone can feel the impact of technology in their own little patch, whether for good or ill. It is harder to see its wider or long-term implications, and harder still to make wise judgements when faced with the pressures of international competition in a world which is one, yet divided.

In such a complex situation all international bodies have a responsibility to help in the process of mutual understanding. Churches especially ought to show the way by mutual sharing, by a special concern for the weak, the backward, and the poor and by a constant insistence on the importance of people and the priority of human values. The bonds of Christian friendship between individuals, parishes, and dioceses, should help to remove fear, ignorance, and suspicion of one another's motives. Above all, the world needs a sign that the barriers of wealth, and the difference between societies in different states of development, can be transcended. For instance, concern about fair prices for raw materials ought to be one of the fruits of membership of the Christian family. If the Church can combine this witness with a constant reminder that technological and economic problems are also human problems, which must not be dealt with in isolation from their impact on the total human community, it will be doing a notable service.

Exhortations to wealthy nations to adjust their economies in favour of poor ones fall on deaf ears, especially when the wealthy nations themselves are suffering from internal strains. Nevertheless it must be said, again and again, the exploitation of the poor is wrong, yet continues on a massive scale. Those who have expertise in economic affairs have a duty to work for effective means of creating a more just and equitable economic order. And the Churches must strive to produce a moral atmosphere in which imaginative programmes of restraint and mutual sharing become politically possible. 'Economics as if people mattered' is not a wild dream, but a vital principle for those who believe that people matter to God.

Part of the witness of the Church in the face of technology is to go on asserting permanent truths about the priority of people over things and of the personal over the impersonal. Belief in the sinfulness of human beings and in the Gospel of redemption and new hope in Christ should enable Christians to avoid the extremes of optimism about what technology can contribute to human happiness and of pessimism about a technological doomsday.

Those whose responsibilities and expertise in many walks of life force them to wrestle with practical problems need a setting, which only the Churches can provide, in which they can find renewal and support, a fresh perspective, a cure for defeatism, and a constant reminder that this is God's world and that without him human activity is ultimately futile. Humanly speaking this is what worship ought to do for us. Churches which provide such a setting and then encourage their members to go out and be involved in the varied problems of the workaday world, are effectively bringing Christian resources to bear on them.

There are times and occasions, though—and their frequency varies in different settings—when the steady witness of the Church to Christian truth and values, and the resources of strength made available in worship, are not an adequate response to the issues of the day. A Church which never speaks or acts on such issues loses credibility and fails its members by offering no guidance. Equally, a Church which speaks or acts in complex matters which have not been fully understood loses credibility in another way and may mislead its members.

We would encourage Christians, therefore, to inform themselves on these matters, to take a full part in inter-disciplinary discussions, and to try to bring to them a deep sense of the value and possibilities of human life, of the ethical and religious dimension in all human activities, and of the wholeness of God's world. We commend resolutions 1 and 2 to the attention of all our readers.

G. Christianity and politics

Underlying all our discussion on the subject of Christianity and politics is the truth that the Church is God's creation. But the world is also God's creation; he made it; he came into it in the person of his Son—he has a plan and a final purpose for it. These truths of creation, incarnation, and consummation demand that the Church be concerned for the world and for people; for the quality of life they live as well as for the response they make to God.

Politics is concerned with power and with the shaping of our societies and their institutions. This is where Christianity and politics meet. For who has the ultimate power over people and what should now be shaping human lives and destinies? We believe that Jesus is Lord and that God has shown us his purposes of justice for human life on earth. Consequently, the Church has a responsibility to declare that purpose, to work out its implications, and to seek to effect its implementation.

To lay down a blueprint for this implementation is impossible and arrogant. Situations vary greatly. In some countries governments ask Church leaders for opinions and even advice. In others the Church is simply neglected, while in yet others it is forbidden to teach even its own people. Obviously understanding love must be extended towards those in other countries who make different political responses from our own.

There are other difficulties. No element of life is completely independent of another. Thus a decision to irrigate land in one locality may mean the abandonment of a water supply scheme in another; the investment of money in a company producing luxury goods may increase employment but also increase people's greed; the goods bought in one country—locally made or imported—affect the economies and work-force of other countries. We cannot arrive at political understanding or at political decisions without a readiness to face complicated questions.

Christians must develop understanding of the 'global village' concept. There is a human solidarity of people on this earth. We are one people created by one God and our responsibility extends to all. This requires determined efforts to gather information as to the ramifications of government policies on the quality of life of people in both our own and other countries. We see the United Nations, with all its defects, as a hopeful sign pointing towards an emerging family of nations, living together harmoniously under law; and we urge Christians to pray and work for the United Nations and for the ideals for which it stands.

In the tradition of the prophets, of John the Baptist, and of Jesus Christ, Church leaders must call and mould the Church to live justly and righteously within itself. As a body the Church should reflect the just, caring, and loving community which is God's desire for humanity.

But Christians may go further. As there is occasion they are to witness to the body politic, pointing out God's ways to mankind, drawing attention to opportunities of reconciliation, and growing together and calling into question policies which adversely affect the quality of life.

Support and encouragement are also to be given to individual Christians to question their own value systems, life-styles, and business dealings. Christians are to be urged to be involved in political parties where this is appropriate, trying to influence formulation of policy and choice of candidates. Support and encouragement are needed too to help them bring to bear on politicians whatever influence they have. The ballot box and personal contact both have their place here. The individual's Christianity is to be lived out in the market place as well as the Church, in relation to one's inter-continental neighbours as well as those in the next house.

In discussion we have drawn back from advocating as a political instrument the way of violence, either by a government or by those opposing the government. Violence begets violence and human life is devalued. We recognize, however, that in situations where injustice has been built into political structures, threatening people with perpetual suppression, Christians may feel that non-violent resistance is no longer the appropriate response and physical violence is the only way to intervene on behalf of the oppressed (see resolution 5).

We also see a need to stress the true nature of the governmental role. It is to serve the nation, not to enhance the position and power of its members; it is to act impartially to achieve the well-being of all; it is to be part of God's plan for order and justice in society.

The Scriptures call on Christians to respect governments, to pray for rulers, but also to 'obey God rather than men'. The State has a true and proper role but its authority over the individual can never be absolute.

A note on Marxism

The issues of the relationship between Christianity and Marxism and of the conflicts between them are of particular political and human importance. Both put forward universal claims about the hopes and the future of mankind and about the world in which we live and what that world should be like.

To face this challenge we must be prepared to recognize that Marxism at its best is concerned with human issues which no Christian can ignore. These include, among many:

1. The gross inequality in the enjoyment of the resources and products of the world both between individuals and groups in a society and between societies.
2. The importance of structures in forming the minds and shaping the destinies of those subjected to them.
3. The widespread sense of helplessness engendered by the failure of politics and institutions (including ecclesiastical institutions) to provide a compelling objective for mankind or a realistic programme for striving after it.

Marxism is attractive to many, because it has a passion for people's welfare, a sense of the sins of society and of the powerful, and an absolute conviction that history has a purpose which can be related to human fulfilment. In these ways it can be said to have the support of Scripture.

We must be careful, therefore, to avoid labelling every radical critique of society and of issues within society (especially criticisms to do with ownership, control, and manipulation of truth) as 'Communist', thereby implying that it is wrong and that the capitalist alternative is both right and Christian. For to use the term 'Communist' purely as one of abuse and rejection is to avoid the many just criticisms which should be seen as reflecting the judgement of God, and to ensure that many positive forms of protest and of reformation, as well as those put forward by Marxists, are stifled.

Christians must also recognize the mistakes of Marxism—its godlessness, its rejection of revelation, its ultimately degrading view of man as no more than a creature of economic circumstances, its motivation of hatred towards those of a different 'class', its fear of the dissident and nonconformist. The Church should not lend unthinking support to anti-Communist campaigns. Both Marxism and capitalism have made promises that have been unfulfilled. Those who believe in God and his Kingdom are called to an even-handed criticism of the sins of society and of themselves under whatever system men and women are living. In place, therefore, of an automatic and unthinking rejection of 'Communism', the Church should identify itself far more with the poor and voiceless and consider afresh its attitude to those who own and control things. How do we express a compassion for people? What is *our* programme of social reform?

Ideologies of the Left and the Right, of the so-called Communist world and the so-called Capitalist world, are both distorted by, and bound up with, power politics. Christians, equipped to offer a positive critique of both, can maintain a dialogue that reaffirms the values which both often appear to deny such as:

1. the reality of God as the centre of human aspiration and history;
2. the constant importance of people in all economic and social planning;
3. the significance of non-economic elements in the construction and working of society and the independent values attested to and expressed through such human activities as art, morality, and religion;
4. the priority of responsible freedom in human affairs, especially as an ability to make effectual choices;
5. the important presence of a dimension in human experience which cannot be wholly expressed in, or satisfied through, material possessions.

Since the Lambeth Fathers last addressed themselves to this question (in 1948) there have been two major changes. An increasing number of our brethren now live in Marxist states. Marxism itself has ceased to be a monolithic system.

In view of the very different circumstances in which our various Churches find themselves, we need to develop means for an exchange of information between our different countries about the necessities, perplexities, and possibilities of our varying political and social situations.

H. Human rights and the dignity of men and women

Christian understanding of human dignity and freedom derives from the biblical concept that Man—male and female—is made in the image of God. This image, obscured in human experience by the fact of sin and estrangement, has been realized in the person of Jesus Christ. He perfects humanity by his obedience to God and sacrificial self-gift to his fellowmen, and offers, through the relationship with himself established in baptism, the opportunity of restoring the image of God in fallen humanity. Christians know from this relationship that God's will and purpose is that all men and women should have equal dignity.

Inherent, therefore, in the Christian tradition is the right to freedom and the responsibility to guarantee and strive for freedom for all persons.

The Declaration of Human Rights adopted by the United Nations spells out some of these rights. The official teaching of the Roman Catholic Church is set out in 'The Church and Human Rights' (Rome, 1975). Other Churches have published similar documents, and those nations who, having subscribed to the Declaration of Human Rights, have taken as a stated goal of their national policy, the guarantee of these rights, are to be commended.

Christians, although they agree that human dignity carries with it human rights for all, have often failed to accord these rights even in their own communities and there is no political structure in existence whose record in terms of human rights is unblemished. In some environments the enjoyment of rights is limited to particular social or ethnic groups or those who accept the political positions of the ruling party or system. Those who question that position may thereby forfeit their rights or opportunities. Similarly in many places the 'haves' are zealous to maintain their own 'rights', but their zeal does not extend to the 'have nots'.

The Christian Church is bound to strive for the realization of full human rights and freedom for all people, and in her history some groups or individuals have brought about great advance in these matters through their convictions and commitment.

Local and national Churches, with the active support of the universal Church, should strive for the incarnation of these rights within their situations, remembering that it is not enough simply to make general statements or to win partial victories. Our aim is freedom for every part of the community and for the creation of those realities of justice and compassion which guarantee that freedom (see resolution 3).

In this, as in all things, Jesus is our guide. He challenged many accepted positions of his day. He died in his struggle to set people free and he rose victorious, transforming his Cross into a symbol of hope and life. In our relationship to this risen Christ, we have peace and freedom which enables us to work with him for peace, freedom, and dignity for all human beings. If these are denied by the State, we, his followers, have no recourse but to obey God rather than any human authority. There have been many confessors and martyrs in our time. Jesus himself warns and affirms us: 'In the world you will have tribulation, but be of good cheer; I have overcome the world' (John 16. 33).

We have been talking about social and political freedom. There is a freedom of spirit which is God's instant gift to those who believe in Christ, and without which social and political freedom will not fulfil the yearnings of our nature. We rejoice that many Christian witnesses in our day have found and demonstrated this freedom of spirit even under severe persecution, and to those who have comparative social and political freedom, we would say, 'All freedom carries responsibility, and the fullness of freedom is found in perfect service of God and man'.

5. The Holy Spirit and the Church today

We have listed some of the urgent issues and problems with which the Church and the individual Christian is faced in today's world. The list is by no means complete. As the Church, we have to live with these issues, and find ways of obedience and witness to God through them. The comments we have been able to work out together reflect clearly the inadequacy of our resources for this task, as well as the seriousness of the challenges the issues pose. Nonetheless, we see no grounds for fear or despair. Although our insufficiency is obvious, we look to God's sufficiency both to lead us into a deeper awareness of what we have to face and to provide us with the resources with which to respond. This sufficiency of God is mediated to us through the Holy Spirit, who is both the divine agent by whom God's will is accomplished in all creation and life, and the one by whom Jesus Christ discerned and obeyed the will of his Father. In all generations this same Spirit is given to the Church to guide, strengthen, and purify it so that it becomes truly the Body of Christ, continuing the task of reconciling all creation to God, and subjecting it to his rule and authority in Christ's name.

So it is that we praise God and thank him for the influence of the renewal movements on the life of the Church today. In recent years we have seen increased instances of parish life being renewed; of individual ministries becoming effective agencies of God's power to heal and to reconcile; of witness to the Christian faith, and of the proclamation of the Gospel with converting power over individuals, communities, and institutions. We rejoice at the abundant evidence from many parts of the world that new forms of the Holy Spirit's gifts and fruit are being bestowed to cleanse, sustain, empower, reconcile, and build up the Body of Christ.

We welcome the signs of God's Spirit within the many and varied expressions of the Church's unity among Christians, and rejoice at the new forms of Christian communal life springing up, and for Christian witness on behalf of world peace and Christian involvement in the struggle for freedom and human dignity for all.

We are also aware of the need for more Christians, Churches, and congregations to expose themselves to these influences of the Holy Spirit's work, and therefore recall the whole Church to a new openness to the renewing power of the Holy Spirit.

At the same time we recognize that there are certain ways in which this Spirit-filled life and activity is either misunderstood or misrepresented.

We are concerned when the Church's preoccupation with its own domestic life results in an insensitivity to the fresh pointings and imperatives of the Spirit in the social order—amid a world struggling for justice, the abolition of war, an equitable distribution of resources, and enough food for all.

We are concerned that conflict which is disgraceful for Christians occurs too often in the life of the Church when one party or another within the fellowship claims exclusively for itself the mind of the Spirit. We particularly caution that the experience which many understand as 'baptism in the Spirit' should not be seen as the only validating experience of Christian renewal. A further pastoral problem arises when a person baptized in infancy experiences the renewing power of the Spirit as an adult, and asks to be baptized again. Such a request must be declined, as it suggests that the efficacy of baptism lies in its effects on the individual's feelings, and denies the fact that baptism incorporates the person who receives it into Christ. Some other form of public affirmation of the renewal is required to meet this pastoral need.

We mention one other matter for concern. Holy Scripture teaches us to test prophecies and other spiritual manifestations (e.g. 1 Thess. 5. 21 and 1 John 4. 1) to determine whether they are indeed of God. Individuals and groups within the Church should be cautious, therefore, before they embrace interpretations which run counter to the *consensus fidelium* which has emerged out of Scripture, tradition, and reason.

In citing these problems, we nevertheless reaffirm that God the Spirit is the author, not of uniformity, but of a rich diversity that exists within an overall unity.

To ensure that this diversity is an enrichment of the life of the Church, we conclude by offering the following guidance:

1. Share fully and faithfully in the balanced liturgical life of the local parish church. Informal services of prayer and praise need this enrichment.

2. Accompany reading and meditation of the Bible with appropriate study of scholarly background material so that the Scripture is understood in its proper context.

3. Search out ways to identify with those who suffer and are poor, being involved personally in efforts to minister to their condition.

4. Remember always that the road from Palm Sunday to Pentecost must pass through Good Friday and Easter. Your calling as a Christian is to be faithful, not necessarily successful (see resolution 7).

Section 2
The people of God and ministry

Chairman: Bishop Douglas Hambidge
Vice-chairman: Archbishop Moses Scott
Secretary: Fr Austin Masters

The following report has the authority only of the section by which it was prepared and endorsed. The Conference as a whole is responsible only for the resolutions printed on pp. 33–52 of this volume; see the statement on authority on p. 5 above.

1. Bishops
2. Ordained ministry
3. Lay ministry
4. Urban and rural ministry
5. Training for ministry
6. Ministry in the context of other faiths and religions
7. Mission and evangelization
8. Liturgy and worship

(For a list of groups and topics, see pp. 28–29 above; for the members of this section in their various groups, see the final column of the lists on pp. 15–26.)

The people of God and ministry

1. Bishops

A. Episcopal authority and synodical government

All authority comes from God and that which is given to the Church involves all the people of God in responsibility and obedience. The bishop derives his authority from the Church, which is the Body of Christ. Christ is the head of the body, the faithful are the members. The bishop receives his authority from both Head and members, and neither without the other. This authority is not to be exercised apart from the Church, that is, without collegial consultation at proper times with brother bishops, and without ensuring that it has the support and consent of the rest of the Church as far as possible. This authority cannot be evident in its fullness as long as the Church is divided. The bishop does not receive his authority by any succession independent of the Church.

Decisions which affect the faith and order of the whole body involve a process which demands the study, prayer, and witness of every member. Since such decisions are subject to human frailties they must always be regarded as provisional, awaiting the continuing judgement of the Holy Spirit expressed by the *consensus fidelium* as to whether they live or die. These decisions call for patience and loving acceptance of those who hold different viewpoints rather than reaction which could lead to schism.

The bishop both exercises and works with different forms of authority. These are:

1. the authority of (a) Holy Scripture and (b) tradition;
2. moral authority;
3. the authority of the office;
4. the authority of counsel by scholars and experts;
5. the law of the Church.

His authority must be always exercised as by a servant in love, humility, and self-abandonment (see the report of the 1948 Lambeth Conference, pt II pp. 84–6). It must however be recognized that there may be cases of defianceof canonical regulations which are so serious and so disruptive of the peace and fellowship of the Christian community that, when all other means have failed, recourse must be made to the machinery provided by canon law for the resolving of the issues.

Within the diocese, the bishop's authority is interpreted and expressed in the missionary pastoral situations, liturgical and teaching activities, and through his leadership and participation in the synods and councils of the Church.

The guardianship of the faith is a collegial responsibility of the episcopate. Synodical government should make provision for this responsibility to be fulfilled. We emphasize the importance of the continuance of Lambeth Conferences whereby the bishops of the Anglican Communion may exercise this collegiality (see resolution 13).

Anglicanism has firmly committed itself to constitutional episcopacy in which the government of the Church by the bishop is limited and supported by synods, canons, and other methods whereby the whole Church—clergy and laity—participate in its government and mission.

The bishop is the sign and agent of unity and continuity within the diocese and within the whole Church.

B. The bishop's function in the Church

The bishop is primarily a father in God to his diocese and he represents to the diocese God's loving care for his family. This ministry is given to him sacramentally within the fellowship of the Church through the laying on of hands by other bishops in succession to Christ the original Apostle. The bishop represents also the apostleship of Christ and as such he ordains to the ministry of the Church.

The primary function of the bishop is to minister in and to the Church which is sent by God to bear witness to the life-giving power of the Gospel of Jesus Christ.

It is also his function to teach, in fulfilling which it is his responsibility to organize the teaching of the faith effectively for the life and witness of his people.

In his function of exercising pastoral care over his diocese, it is necessary for him so to discharge his own pastoral care of his clergy that they in turn are truly pastors of the flock committed to him and them. When he delegates pastoral responsibility to the clergy he must do so in such a way and in such a spirit that they in turn will delegate responsibility to those who work with them.

The bishop represents his individual diocese within the Church of God in his meetings with his fellow bishops. In return, he represents the universal episcopate to his own people, and is at once the focus and symbol of the catholicity of the Church.

Again, it is the function of the bishop to exercise a prophetic ministry to the world. To do so requires consultation about the situation and about the most effective method of doing so (see resolution 18).

The function of a bishop, therefore, does not cease with his personal ministry of ordaining, preaching, teaching, pastoral oversight, and public pronouncements. It extends also to the oversight of these functions in the diocese at large, not in a bureaucratic way but as the head of the family with concern for each member.

C. Training of bishops

The Lambeth 1968 Report (p. 109) said 'bishops should have opportunities of undertaking a course of training for their office. Where such training cannot be provided within a regional Church, it is to be hoped that the Anglican Consultative Council will make the necessary provision for bishops from a wider area.'

Training can never be a substitute for vocation: the acquisition of skills alone does not make a bishop. Professional training cannot replace that mysterious and gracious empowering by the Holy Spirit which is the Father's gift for ministry. A bishop's life needs, therefore, to be ever open to the guiding and transforming activity of the Holy Spirit. A specific course of training for his work then becomes an aspect of this vulnerability.

Most bishops at present have to learn their job as they go along, without training. In order to implement the hope expressed by the Lambeth Conference of 1968 and referred to above, the following recommendations are made (see resolution 19):

1. That written guidelines be prepared for episcopal training, to include the bishop's role and relationships, and his spiritual and family life. This would show *what* a bishop needs to learn.

2. That member Churches of the Anglican Communion prepare their own versions of these guidelines in order to cover the training requirements of bishops' functioning in their particular circumstances. This would show *how* to apply what a bishop needs to learn.

3. That a general (but not exhaustive) table of contents for the initial guidelines would be:

a. Clarification of the episcopal office

1. the office of bishop in the Church of God;

2. the role and function of the bishop in the Church.

b. Personal growth and life-style

1. maintaining vital dependence on God (prayer, study, meditation);

2. spiritual growth and development in the face of new situations and changing value systems;

3. development of support systems—family, friends, peers, community;

4. time management for re-creation and care of family, friends, personal health;
5. continuing education.

c. Operational skills

1. Liturgical	
2. Administrative	organizational personnel financial legal
3. Role fulfilment	goal setting team building accountability evaluation

It is impossible to separate a bishop's public office from his private and domestic life. It is important that care be taken to safeguard this wholeness. Four areas, therefore, need careful attention:

1. *Integration of knowledge and contemplation.* That his intellectual and devotional life are so developed that he is able to make meaning of crisis, be critically conscious of social injustice, and make intellectual sense out of seemingly disparate circumstances. Adequate attention to physical and emotional health must also be considered.

2. *Intimate family integration* (or, if single, its equivalent). A sound home situation to rely on for support, and deep mutual sharing in an atmosphere of personal trust.

3. *Team integration.* A good 'give and take' working group in which the bishop can participate effectively as member and leader, and which provides him with adult-to-adult interaction.

4. *Integration with equals.* Solid group support from other executive leaders (not necessarily episcopal) with whom he can share the concerns of work and family.

2. Ordained ministry

A. Growth and understanding of self-supporting ministries

Almost as many different patterns of self-supporting ministry seem to be developing as there are provinces in the Anglican Communion. They vary from the priest who receives limited monetary support from Church funds and is provided with land on which to grow food for sustenance, to the priest who devotes spare time from a secular occupation to serve in a non-stipendiary capacity in a specific parochial situation. There are many other variations.

The exercise of these ministries seems so far to have been largely concerned with providing, or assisting, what has been the traditional pattern of a parochial ministry. There is, however, growing evidence of new patterns of ministry being exercised by self-supporting priests. Among these there are those whose ministry is specifically within the places of their own secular employment. These are those trained and ordained to minister in 'house-church' situations in densely populated and secularized urban areas. There are those chosen to minister in isolated communities or sometimes in ethnic groups which otherwise would not receive the pastoral and sacramental ministry of a priest. There are those being ordained and equipped to serve if the Church is forced underground. Reports of such developments make it clear that there is an increasing use of new patterns of ordained ministry to serve in situations where the traditional forms are inadequate.

If the Church is to be open to the world and its needs, such new patterns of ministry are inevitable. It is important that there should be flexibility in their extension and development. This will require episcopal support and encouragement, particularly where situations arise for which existing synodical rules make no provision. The ecumenical opportunities of this wider ministry must not be neglected.

We endorse pp. 102ff. of the report of the Lambeth Conference of 1968 and p. 49 of the report of the third (Trinidad, 1976) meeting of the Anglican Consultative Council regarding selection, training and post-ordination training, and pastoral care. We recognize that this ministry requires special gifts in the candidate, special training, and strong pastoral support after ordination.

It is therefore important that all self-supporting priests are related to diocesan life. Where possible they should be part of a team, particularly in the early years following ordination. Those who work in isolated situations especially need the support of a worshipping community and the opportunity to discuss and evaluate their work.

It is also important to recognize the obligations the self-supporting priest has both to family and employer. To neglect such responsibilities undermines the priest's integrity. There will be strains and risks. It is here that pastoral oversight has to be provided.

We see a demanding and vital role for the bishops not only in providing such oversight in relation to these ministers but also in serving as the focus of unity for the several patterns of ordained ministry which may emerge.

B. Ordination of women to the priesthood

Ministry of women

Resolution 38 of the Lambeth Conference of 1968 declared in specific terms a commitment to a full participation by the women of the Church in all liturgical functions open to lay men. We endorse that commitment, symbolizing as it does,

1. our recognition of the very great contribution that has been made, and is being made, by women in the total life of the Church;
2. our conviction that only as women are fully accepted as members of the Body of Christ in its mission and ministry can it be said that the Body is moving towards completeness; and
3. that the specific ministries open to women in the Church should enable them to exercise their distinctive gifts.

Women in the diaconate
We have not given particular examination to the issue of the diaconate. Some members are looking for change along the lines of resolution 32 of the Lambeth Conference of 1968, and it is suggested that those member Churches which do not ordain women as deacons should now make the necessary changes to enable them to do so, rather than ordaining them to a separate order of deaconesses (see resolution 20).

Women and the priesthood
The ordination of women to the priesthood is an accomplished fact in some of our Provinces; others have opposed it; others again foresee its happening, but not yet. Underlying the decisions of synods there are serious questionings of conscience on all sides arising out of deep theological conviction. A pressing issue before this Conference has been how to establish ways of guarding the unity of our Communion, and of sustaining each other. We note the 'conscience clause' in the appropriate legislation of the Anglican Church of Canada as providing a helpful model in this respect.

We judge that resolution 21 of this Conference provides as appropriate basis for ordering relationships between Provinces and dioceses in the given situation, and expresses a common concern for Anglican unity.

We are concerned about the pastoral needs of women:

1. ordained to the priesthood in present circumstances of less than universal acceptance; and
2. of those denied ordination solely because they are women though convinced of their vocation;

and we urge our Provinces and dioceses to be especially sensitive to them.

We are also concerned that the women described in 1 and 2 above be sensitively aware of the peculiarly delicate state of affairs and discussion within and between the Provinces and dioceses of our Communion; and that they should make their own contributions, by God's grace, to its healing and strengthening.

We are also equally concerned about those who remain as loyal members of the Church and who are opposed to the ordination of women to the priesthood, as we are with those who support it. We wish to affirm wholeheartedly that the good standing of both in the Church is in no way impaired, and that all retain every right to full participation in its life, ministry, and mission.

We acknowledge the opinions expressed to us by spokesmen of other Churches. We hope that they will bear with us as we try to respond to the opportunities of dialogue concerning those matters which divide us (see resolution 21).

Women and the episcopate

It is clear that the prospect of the consecration of women to the episcopate is an element in the present situation and we therefore draw attention to resolution 22 of this Conference. We hope that this, together with the general approach to the ordination of women we have outlined, will enable this particular issue of consecration to the episcopate to be approached with discretion and mutual respect.

3. Lay ministry

The Christian ministry is committed to the whole people of God; and not, as is often believed, to the ordained ministry alone. The section therefore reiterates what has long been said on this subject because there are still many places in our Communion in which this complementarity of ministry of clergy and laity is not being demonstrated.

There are, however, clear signs that God is calling and equipping his people for their true tasks. Clergy need to recognize this movement of the Spirit, to facilitate it and encourage their people to respond to it; lay folk need to recognize and use the gifts God is giving them.

The laity have unique ability and opportunity by word and deed to bring Christian insights and the Christian faith to people with whom they live and work, in home and family, whether at the place of manual toil, or on the company board. They go where the clergy do not go, and speak where the clergy are not heard. It is important that the clergy encourage the fullest exercise of genuinely lay responsibility for the enrichment of the whole community. This will help to avoid any danger of clericalizing leading lay people, and also of the clergy feeling themselves threatened.

'No one wants untrained troops. Anglicans pay lip service to training' (report of the Lambeth Conference of 1968, p. 97). The first statement remains true. For the second, while we must never be complacent about it, the new and imaginative ways in which training has begun to take place over the last ten years can be thankfully recognized. Churches in the developing countries in particular are leading the way as they respond to the exciting challenges presented to them. Churches with more ancient traditions are finding ways of release from those rigidities which have restricted their life.

From the world around us comes the possibility of added efficiency in methods of organization, new skills in understanding the working of groups, enhanced development of training procedures. The Church will be well advised to pay heed to all of these. It should also plan such training ecumenically wherever possible.

But training procedures are not enough in themselves. As the Church draws upon the living spiritual heritage of its past, and discovers new realms of spirituality, every member depends directly on Christ, the only source of life, who alone can make training effective in bringing life to others.

Note on lay presidency at the Eucharist

During the Conference an additional group of bishops from section 2 was formed 'to look at the arguments for lay members of the Church being licensed to preside at the Eucharist in special circumstances'. In their report they held that where it is not possible to provide a president the bishop is still responsible for making the sacrament of Holy Communion available, and they believed that there might be circumstances in which it would be justifiable for him to authorize a lay member to preside in his name providing such a person had the support of the local congregation. They recommended that where there was need, particular members of local congregations should be authorized to preside at the Eucharist under certain specified conditions.

When the report was presented to the section it was decided that the subject should not be further discussed.

4. Urban and rural ministry

A. Urban ministry

In one sense most of developed society can be described as urban. But there are particular comments to be made about big cities of half a million or more, which take on an altogether different character from smaller communities. Such a modern city can be a place of hope: it can also be a place of despair. In Europe and North America our Church has found it harder to root itself among the urban 'losers' than in any other social grouping. In fast-growing cities of Latin America, Africa, and Asia, many first-generation migrants keep their links with their village or tribe; but those ties are likely to be broken in subsequent generations.

People will not understand who our Lord is through words and worship alone. The unspoken assumptions, which mould Christians' behaviour, speak more loudly than their words. Jesus knew this well enough; he pointed to and acted out the Kingdom of God. The preaching of Christ comes from within a visible community. That community is called to be catholic, reaching across the barriers of class and race. We can never be ultimately content if the Church lives separate lives in homogeneous ethnic or class groups, however much their numbers may grow. The city of man needs to see that the community of faith provides a model of harmonious diversity.

The greatest resource which the Church has in order to serve God in the city is quite simply the Christian people there who worship and are disciples. True worship, evangelization, and discipleship will lead to personal encounter with Christ and with people in all sectors of life. Urban people live their lives in differing environments and Christ's disciples must seek to penetrate each of them. They will include:

commerce and industry
the caring professions
community life both where people reside and elsewhere
politics at all levels
leisure interests.

Christians, along with others, often feel alone in these situations; so they often do nothing, when a word or an action for truth and justice is needed. They need to join hands with other people of good will. But they also need support from diocesan resources and from other ministries of the wider Church, such as industrial mission.

If there is any reduction in numbers or in money, the Church should give priority of resources to the unchurched mission areas of cities. They should be able to provide their own ministries from within, reversing the assumption that the parish which can pay receives the available manpower. However, the clergy going into the cities are likely to need training in fresh skills.

The Christian prophetic ministries reflect in the city the character of the God who is just. This means a positive commending of what is believed to be right in our society as much as criticism of what is believed to be wrong. Christians are called to challenge racial prejudice, denial of civil rights, poor facilities, or the often-accepted wisdom of making our resources available only to the well-integrated, the adept, or the successful.

The skills of all professional people must be used co-operatively to work for economic and social justice for all the city's inhabitants and not for a privileged few. Christians need to bring a vision of the whole—for the whole of each person's life, and for the whole of a city's life. Those in responsible positions need to live in the Gospel spirit of hope. Their expertise and commitment to the city can play a part in its regeneration. All professionals, including clergy, need to know when to get out of the way. Lay ministry in the city does not only belong to the educated; sometimes change will be brought about from below, and the vital influencers will not have any obvious rank or qualification. God can raise up responsible, indigenous leadership for both Church and secular life in any community in the world.

B. Rural ministry

Not only historically, but in present actuality, the rural Church in our various countries has a significant role to play in the life of the whole Church. We affirm this against suggestions that rural communities and the rural Church demand only secondary attention.

Not all rural societies are thinly populated and diminishing, with village life decaying. In those that are, we note a special challenge to the faith and vision and creativity in ministry of the clergy. The rural clergy need special skills, and to be special kinds of people. The attention of seminaries is particularly drawn to the peculiarities in culture and in skills demanded in the training of those who will minister in rural parishes, whilst the attention of the bishops is drawn to the special needs of the rural clergy for refresher courses and continuing support. The tensions that isolation and loneliness often impose on the families of the clergy in some rural settings must be recognized and provision made for special support for clergy wives and children in these situations.

Having all this in mind, the responsibility of the local Christian community is to be involved in, to support, to initiate, and where conscience demands to oppose government policies, legislation, and administration that affect the life of the community: for example, pressures that are eroding the family farms and family businesses in many areas; lack of employment opportunities that drive people, particularly the young, to the cities to look for work; relative lack of welfare, educational, and recreational facilities.

In older-established Church areas the legacies of history bear heavily against introducing necessary changes. In other areas some are confronted with establishing a viable Christian community in an entirely fresh setting, with few or no inherited resources, and often among an apathetic or hostile society. In both situations the challenge to proclaim the Gospel is critical. In all such situations, concern about training and formation of Christian membership and leadership should be high.

In parts of Africa, some bishops are giving what they feel to be a disproportionate amount of time and energy to the work of confirming. Many bishops labour under an absence of adequate support staff, programme facilities, and money. Most must give undue time and energy to travel. How far is this aggravated by a constraint to administer the diocese on traditional lines? What is needed is a model or concept of parish ministry that breaks loose from the traditional English parochial system to which most of us are heirs.

The following recommendations are made for rural Churches:

1. Local congregations should be regarded as 'ministry centres' in which the emphasis is on equipping the laity for effective ministry *within the Church and in society*.

2. In regard to personnel, the 'total ministry' concept is commended, i.e. every member is regarded as a minister, and there is a wide range of ministries to be exercised, beginning with the ordained ministry and extending to lay ministries, both stipendiary and non-stipendiary.

3. In the bishop's ministry there should be special emphasis on his priorities. He should be free to delegate to others any duties which are not essential to the exercise of his special episcope.

4. In some areas the traditional practice of confirmation places a heavy burden on bishops, therefore it is recommended that each province of the Anglican Communion should re-examine the theology and practice of initiation with particular reference to the bishop's role.

5. Training for ministry

The task of training for ministry is to recognize and draw out, refine and discipline the talents God invests in men and women. To take advantage of theological education is both a right and a responsibility for every Christian. Since the gifts required are already implanted by God, the work of equipping for ministry begins with discernment; by sharpening the self-awareness of everyone's potential; by helping everyone to discover, identify, and exercise ministry within his or her daily work.

Equipping Christians for ministry will mean helping them to think theologically; helping them to examine and develop their gifts in the light of God's own activity. This is a life-long process which may and should be nurtured in a variety of ways; but at the heart of such equipping is the need for regular sacramental nourishment, prayer, Bible study, and meditation.

In responding to the challenge of nurturing this life-long process, we urge upon the Church the need to take more account of the educational principles which should underlie all kinds of equipping for ministry.

In many parts of the world today, sensitivity and imagination are essential if truth is to be imparted, faith shared, and love ministered. Where these gifts are presented insensitively or arrogantly those gifts will be more often left than taken. There will, of course, remain situations in which the simple handing out of information continues to be important. But the teaching process has always depended on a two-way relationship between teacher and learner. This in itself encourages self-awareness. We believe this phenomenon is, increasingly, becoming better understood.

Equipping for ministry within the Christian Church requires in the first place an awareness of the personality, talents, and life-experience of the learner. The resources of teachers and learners then become an instrument through which the Christian heritage is explored and appropriated. In this connection we believe there is clear evidence that where lay people and the ordained train side by side, their complementary roles are sharpened into focus rather than blurred into confusion.

Awareness of culture and environment is also important if the proper methods and techniques are to be applied in each place. Thus we look for ways which will help the learner to develop his or her ways of theological thinking appropriate to the kind of ministry which is to be exercised. Teacher and learner alike need to understand in depth and with precision the different stages of emotional and intellectual development in the whole learning experience, and thus to match material and method to these stages.

All these criteria should be borne in mind as we consider the use both of traditional methods of training (e.g. group Bible study) and of new developments (e.g. Theological Education by Extension which uses correspondence material, cassette, or broadcast material in the context of a group brought together for regular seminars).

6. Ministry in the context of other faiths and religions

Population statistics of five of the larger countries in Asia, in which various forms of Hinduism, Buddhism, Taoism, and Confucianism are dominant, raise questions about the mission of the Church. Together they make up approximately one-third of the world's total population.

Japan	1 per cent Christians (0.05 per cent Anglicans)
China	less than 1 per cent Christians
Bangladesh	0.28 per cent Christians
India	2 per cent Christians
Pakistan	1 per cent Christians

Population statistics for other countries in Asia differ in significant ways but they do not contradict the general impression that, except in particular areas, Christians are a small proportion of the total population. In the Episcopal Church in Jerusalem and the Middle East, where Islam is dominant, there are 13.5 per cent Christians (0.01 per cent Anglicans), and in the Sudan 8 per cent Christians (1.08 per cent Anglicans).

Centuries ago, some countries in these areas had a greater proportion of Christians among their inhabitants. Before the advent of Islam the majority of people in Egypt were Christians (now there are less than 10 per cent), and much of North Africa and the Near East were Christian. Moreover, according to tradition, Christians have been present in India since the first century, and between the seventh and fourteenth centuries there were Nestorian bishoprics in Central Asia. The Christian Church has made little progress in these areas, and with the renewal of other faiths some would even speak of declining influence. These facts have to be taken seriously and what God is saying to his Church through them, discovered.

The problem is not simply one of religion. The dominant religions of these areas are expressed in the cultures associated with them, which embody their beliefs, values, customs, and institutions. The Churches often appear to be identified with Western culture, and in some circumstances, despite the existence of ancient Churches as in the Middle East and India, Christianity itself appears to be a foreign religion.

Questions of cultural identity are important also in other parts of the world where there are pluralist societies, both for the Churches and for minorities within predominantly Christian populations. Christians in Britain have a responsibility to act justly and compassionately towards their fellow citizens of other faiths: The Churches of the USA, Canada, Australia, and New Zealand are called to be sensitive towards the needs of the indigenous/aboriginal peoples for affirmation of their cultural identities. In Africa, Islam often appears more congenial to the traditional ways of life and by contrast the main Churches face growing problems because of their past failure (now changing) to accept the traditional arts, music, and customs of their peoples which are the fruit of generations of wisdom and experience.

In the past the barriers between religious communities were such that it was very difficult for people to hear or to understand the teachings of faiths other than their own. This is no longer the case: the communications explosion, modern means of travel, and the growing interdependence of the world economy, make people in many countries aware of alternative patterns of belief and conduct and open to their influence. In some areas, it is possible for people to transfer their allegiance from one religious community to another without undue pressure or difficulty, and members of the same family may belong to different religions. We welcome this new openness. We were also encouraged to hear what some of our number told us about the way in which people of other faiths were turning towards Christ.

Two other factors are important. First, the task of building nation states in the post-colonial, technological world gives many opportunities for Christians to work with others as colleagues together in a common task. Many of the problems, political, social, and economic, are new, and there is much greater mobility and freedom than in earlier periods. Secondly, the development of communications, and the spread of Western education, technology, and language have familiarized the people of other faiths with some Christian values and ideals, even if in a distorted form. The attitudes of Buddhists, Hindus, Muslims, and others towards society, the family, and the individual have changed in recent years. Christians on the other hand, are only at the beginning of recognizing God in other faiths.

For the Christian mission in these circumstances two things are important:

1. Christians are called to bear witness to Jesus Christ, clearly and wholeheartedly.

2. Christians are called to do so as they stand alongside their fellow human beings within the particular environment and society in which they live their common life.

There are many opportunities today for Christians to stand alongside those of other faiths in the many tasks of nation-building, of seeking justice and peace, of working for the realization of the Kingdom of God. A person is not called to deny the values and traditions of his native culture when he becomes a Christian, except when they are in conflict with the essentials of the Gospel. Rather he should glory in them as some of the treasures which will be brought into the City of God at the end of history. Moreover, although he is called to proclaim the Word of God, he may only do so effectively if, like the prophets of old, he is personally identified with the community to which he speaks. It is of the utmost importance for the mission of the Church that Christians should do all they can to express and live out the Gospel in the context of the particular society of which they are members. By sharing in this way with the life of the whole community, Christians will communicate something of the Christian way of life and system of values to those who are not Christians, and will also learn something of the value-systems of others.

In this report, attention is directed mainly to those areas in which other faiths and religions are dominant. But it is not only in them that the Church conducts its mission in the presence of people of other faiths. In the interdependent 'global village' of our times, Christians in every country are neighbours to people who belong to other faiths and ideologies, as well as those who live without religion at all. Every member Church of the Anglican Communion is called to take seriously the question of relationships with people of other faiths and to make more adequate provision for training, for reflection, and for mission in this area.

We recognize and rejoice in our special relationship with the people of the Jewish faith which is based on our common heritage in the Old Testament Scriptures and the mission of Jesus. We deeply regret that discrimination against Jews in practically every country in the past has prevented our dialogue with them from being as fruitful as it might be. We need to discuss with them the significance of the teaching of Jesus, and the relation of Kingship to the service of suffering spoken of in Deutero-Isaiah. This dialogue with Judaism is important not only for its own sake but also because it provides a model by which we may learn to respond to the sacred writings and histories of the other world faiths (see resolution 37 (3)).

The Gospel is good news about the risen Christ who is alive in the midst of the Church and the world. It is made effective in men's lives by the Holy Spirit, whose task it is 'to convince the world and to show where wrong and right and judgement lie' (John 16. 8). Our task is to be servants of God's living Word, and in our particular circumstances to communicate and confirm it to our neighbours. The Gospel is greater than ourselves and our confidence is in God. Our dependence upon the guidance and help of the Holy Spirit was constantly emphasized by the African bishops amongst us.

We have the enduring obligation to proclaim the good news of Jesus Christ. We echo the words of St Paul, 'Necessity is laid upon me: yea, woe is me if I do not evangelize' (1 Corinthians 9. 16). To evangelize, by every means available, is the corporate responsibility of the Church, as integral a part of the life of every congregation as is worship or service or the creation of fellowship. Indeed the evangelistic task is in direct relation to the living Lord who meets with all mankind in the grace and the joy of the sacraments.

In the furtherance of this task of evangelism, every Christian is called to serve God's mission to the world through the whole of his life. In this service, witness and conduct go hand in hand. There should be a clear integrity between the message of liberation, renewal, and re-creation which the Church proclaims and the ordinary daily behaviour of Christians. 'Let your conduct', St Paul said to the Philippians, 'be worthy of the gospel of Christ . . .' (Philippians 1. 27). This witness, however, must be within the particular cultural context in which we live and relevant to it. The witness of conduct must be accompanied by the witness of speech. Again this must be appropriate to the context in which the witness is given: effective witness is given by one person to another in the context of friendship and mutual understanding, within the circumstances of ordinary everyday life (see resolution 36).

The mission of the Church has for long been associated with institutions of learning or of healing.

1. They were founded in the service of the Gospel by people whose motives were those of love. They continue to be one of the ways in which the Church tries to obey our Lord's call that it should be of service to the world. Through these institutions Christians share God's blessing with others.

2. Every institution needs to be fully part of the life of its local Church, and an expression of the service of that Church to the community in which it is set. Such institutions should belong to the local Churches and be integrated into their structures. This raises, however, urgent questions about their support and about the continuing obligation which the whole Church has to maintain them in certain circumstances.

3. Serious questions, however, are now being asked about such institutions in the context of mission and evangelism. Muslims and others believe that many of them have in the past been used improperly in the service of the Gospel. For example, advantage is said to be taken of people's sickness and vulnerability to use their stay in Christian hospitals

as an opportunity to press the Christian message improperly upon their attention. In such circumstances it is believed that the main motive in Christian service is not compassion but the desire to convert people to Christianity (see the October 1976 edition of the *International Review of Mission,* which discusses these issues in the context of Christian-Muslim relations).

The ministry of service should be given simply for love of God and to express his compassion towards those in need, and such ministry should not be used as the primary method of evangelization. Evangelism is, in fact, the responsibility of every member of the Church in the context of their whole lives.

In considering mission towards people of other faiths we need to reflect upon the way in which the first Christians took the Good News from Palestine out into the Hellenistic cities and provinces of the Roman Empire. Not only did they have to use another language (Greek in place of Aramaic), but they also had to use it in a different environment. 'The Acts and the Epistles employ in the expression and commendation of the faith terms consciously drawn from, and directed to, the familiar world of speech and thought among Gentile hearers. It is equally clear that the new borrowings were in studied divergence from basic terms current in the Judean or Galilean context but either opaque or difficult for pagan, Gentile folk' (Kenneth Cragg *Christianity in World Perspective* p. 55). Similar efforts at translation, of words but also of ideas, are called for as Christians try to communicate the Gospel within Taoist, Confucianist, Hindu, Buddhist, Muslim, and other cultures, and within the new technological scientific culture of the twentieth century. All our member Churches should be involved in this work of transposition in ways appropriate to them. It is a theological task of primary importance for the mission of the Church to the world and it deserves much more attention and more resources than have so far been given to it. It is a task for every Christian in one way or another and not simply one for the specialist. It is also a task to which the Anglican Consultative Council called the member Churches in pages 53–54 of the report of its third (Trinidad) meeting in 1976.

'Dialogue in Community'

Our report does not provide a detailed evaluation of other religions as they are in themselves. We refer, however, to the discussion and activity in the field of relationships with people of other faiths going on in many countries, and also at the international level, to the work associated with the World Council of Churches and the Vatican Secretariat for non-Christians. Valuable resources also exist among Anglicans who have lived among those of other faiths for many generations, and we encourage the active participation in this work of member Churches of the Anglican Communion all across the world.

'Dialogue' is one of the key words used in this connection and we wish to make the following brief points about it:

1. 'Dialogue' should not be confused with evangelism. But it also is a way by which Christians may share the Good News about Jesus with those who worship God within another faith.

2. 'Dialogue is a means of living out our faith in Christ in service of community with our neighbours.'[1] It is not an abstract theoretical discussion about theology; at best it is a genuine meeting of particular individuals in the integrity of their personal lives and convictions. Dialogue is not only about religious themes, but may and should be carried out in other spheres of life as well.

3. In dialogue with those of other faiths the Christian asks three questions:

a. What do I see in the faith and life of the other persons which I recognize to be signs of the presence of God among them?

b. What do the other persons say about my own faith and in particular about what appear to them to be its inadequacies or weaknesses?

c. What does God wish to say to us within the context of our common responsibilities and mutual friendship?

4. To engage in open, mutual dialogue with those of other faiths, patiently listening and responding to each other, does not involve the Christian in a denial of the uniqueness of Christ. It should, however, lead him to define that uniqueness in inclusive, rather than in exclusive, terms. The uniqueness of Christ lies in the significance which he has for the whole race of mankind: but we affirm that significance with the humility of Bethlehem and the brokenness of Calvary, as well as in the certainty of Easter Day. We commend resolution 37 to the notice of our readers.

7. Mission and evangelization

Mission means everything for which the Church of God is sent. It is the apostleship of the Church and issues from the apostleship of the Lord: 'As the Father has sent me, even so I send you' (John 20. 21). Evangelization is one of a number of ways in which this mission is carried out. Though not the only way, therefore, it none the less belongs to the heart of the Church's mission (so also the Lausanne Covenant, Pope Paul in *Evangelii nuntiandi,* and the 1975 Nairobi WCC).

The Church is sent with the Gospel to every person: to those in poverty, sickness, oppression, persecution, and any form of suffering as much as to

[1] From the statement of the WCC Consultation at Chiang Mai, Thailand, April 1977.

those ignorant of Christ. To equate evangelistic outreach exclusively with meeting only one form of need is to distort the Gospel. The Church proclaims the victory of Christ over all sin, over all that makes people less than whole.

Evangelization

Jesus is himself the Good News reaching out through us. He is the Lord who is with his Church as he sends it into the world to men and women in bondage of any kind. It is always addressed to people in need, although at the beginning they may be unaware of their need. Effective evangelization requires, on the part of those sent, a decisive identification with and commitment to the Lord and to those to whom they are sent, drawing their attention to the God who through Christ loves and cares for them. The Church also thus challenges them to respond to the Gospel: to know and openly acknowledge Jesus Christ alone to be their Saviour and Lord, to open themselves to the renewing and empowering Spirit of God, and to live within the believing community, sharing in its mission to the world.

Methods of evangelization

Evangelization, as ACC–3 reminded us, is 'the faithful proclamation of the Gospel'. The context will determine what methods are used to gain a hearing for the Gospel. Yet the best form of communication will be sterile unless the Spirit moves the hearers to respond.

Agents of evangelization

1. *The Christian community*. The Church is an agent of the Gospel when it is the kind of community in which fellowship is found both between the members and with their Lord. The problem of evangelization is alienation between people and the Church and the Gospel. Evangelization is 'sharing the Gospel', and the major task of the Church is to gain a hearing. Evangelization means enabling people to respond to the claims of Christ on their lives and the demands of the Gospel for the community and the world. Two things are necessary:

a. The notion that evangelization is the responsibility of selected people within the Church must be rejected. It is a task laid upon all the members of the Christian community. They must learn how to share the Gospel wherever they are; both person-to-person and also within the society where they work.

b. The local Church must define its task within its locality and enable its members for that task. It is the rhythm between sharing the Gospel in the world and being equipped for those tasks in the Christian community, between obedience and nurture, between service and renewal, which will determine the forms and content of Church life.

Thus will the Church be the agent of evangelization, for it will then be structured to minister Christ to the world.

2. *Personal testimony.* A personal word of testimony, witnessing to what Christ has done for, and therefore what he means to, oneself, can often be much more effective than preaching in bringing about a response to the Gospel.

3. *The bishop.* The bishop is deeply concerned with evangelization in his diocese. It is his responsibility to see that the Gospel is proclaimed and so that evangelization is carried out in its totality, both by word and deed relationships. Fellowship with his brother bishops is an important support for the bishop in his evangelistic responsibility.

8. Liturgy and worship

Christian worship is always the action of the ascended Christ, in which the offers himself and his whole Body to the Father in the power of the Holy Spirit. The Eucharist is the heart of Christian worship because it is the showing forth of his death and resurrection until his coming again. Worship is never initiated by human beings. Rather, we are caught up into an on-going action already taking place ('Therefore with angels and archangels and with all the company of heaven. . .').

The Bible teaches that God, because he is holy, requires that those who worship him should be striving both corporately and individually after holiness and justice. In true worship, the whole of life is offered to God.

One of the most important discoveries in the twentieth century is that the earth is a fragile place and that substances basic for survival are not inexhaustible. For Christians the One who died on the Cross is he by whom all things were made. Christian worship needs to reflect the essential goodness of God's creation and the stewardship of it entrusted to us.

There has been a welcome growth in the understanding that worship is a corporate activity in which all members of the Body of Christ have their proper share. To each is given by the Holy Spirit, as St Paul teaches, his or her own gift to be used for the building up of the Body of Christ.

Whenever the individual Christian prays it is as a member of the Body of Christ. Private prayer should be nourished by the corporate worship in which he participates and should in return enliven his share in that worship.

In the past, the Book of Common Prayer was an important unifying factor in Anglican worship. The development of regional Prayer Books in the twenties and thirties and of more thorough-going revisions of the services in recent years has altered the situation. Nevertheless, worship remains an important unifying force, as is evidenced by the remarkable agreement on the structure of the Eucharist that has developed in recent years, not only among the provinces of our own communion but also ecumenically (see resolution 23). We believe this unity in structure can rightly co-exist with flexibility in content and variety in cultural expression, for the Holy Spirit is both a Spirit of order and an unpredictable wind. The existence of this flexibility and variety increases the need for care and thought in the preparation of worship. 'Informal' does not mean 'casual'.

We note that within our structure of the Eucharist, several parts of our Communion have provided a number of alternative Canons (Thanksgivings) to express the range of emphases in understanding of the Eucharist and its use in differing pastoral circumstances. We commend this practice to the consideration of other parts of the Anglican Communion.

We hope that our rich musical heritage will continue to be used both in new and old liturgies. At the same time, composers should be encouraged to provide for the new services worthy musical settings both for choirs and congregations.

The bishop's office is to be the chief liturgical minister in his diocese, and from that comes his general responsibility for the oversight of worship within his jurisdiction. Liturgy is a living thing which grows with the life of the Church. Growth in both individual and corporate prayer is essential and is the work of the Holy Spirit (Rom. 8. 26). We encourage Christians to engage in worship of different kinds in groups of different sizes, e.g. in the intimacy of the small group and in the occasional large or festival gathering. Both of these can complement the regular worship of the congregation.

Section 3
The Anglican Communion in the world-wide Church

Chairman: Bishop Patrick Rodger
Vice-chairman: Archbishop Allen Johnston
Secretary: Archdeacon E. S. Light

The following report has the authority only of the section by which it was prepared and endorsed. The Conference as a whole is responsible only for the resolutions printed on pp. 33–52 of this volume; see the statement on authority on p. 5 above.

1. **The nature and organization of the Anglican Communion**
2. **The Anglican Communion in the *oikoumene***
3. **Evangelization and renewal**

(For a list of groups and topics within Section 3, see p. 29 above; for the members of this section in their various groups see the final column of the lists on pp. 15–26.)

The Anglican Communion in the world-wide Church

1. The nature and organization of the Anglican Communion

At the Lambeth Conference of 1978, to a greater extent than ever, we have seen evidence that the Anglican Communion is in a very real sense a world-wide family. Yet we have had to ask ourselves some searching questions concerning the nature of that which entitles us to describe ourselves as a 'Communion'. Many of the old cultural factors (including the invariable use of the English language) look very different today. In this part of our report, we deal with deeper elements, many of which are the concern of other Christians as well: a doctrinal basis, partnership in mission, and stewardship. Finally we come to a specific treatment of a subject which has naturally occupied our thoughts a good deal, viz: the structures of the Anglican Communion and their development.

A. The basis of Anglican unity

The question is sometimes asked, do the Churches of the Anglican Communion have a distinctive doctrinal basis? This may be answered with an unambiguous affirmative, provided it is realized that what is distinctive is chiefly the patterning of elements shared in common with other Churches.

Statements of doctrinal fundamentals may be found in the constitutional documents and canon law of most of the Churches; this basis is further reinforced by the standard of worship contained in the prayer books in use; it is reflected in repeated statements of the Lambeth Conferences; it is upheld through the common order of the threefold ministry by which particular persons are called to minister the doctrine and sacraments and the discipline of Christ; it is held together by the bond of an episcopal order, as a sign and instrument in space and time of the continuity of the bishops and their Churches with the apostolic community; and it is personally grounded in the loyal relationship of each of the Churches to the Archbishop of Canterbury who is freely recognized as the focus of unity.

Examination of the documents reveals a marked resemblance between the member Churches of the Anglican Communion, such as might characterize the different members of a single family. The family model is appropriate for two reasons. In the first place it implies a form of likeness between the members, which is other than uniformity, but is nonetheless strong enough to hold them together in the midst of strain and tension. It is also appropriate in as much as it illustrates the kind of dispersed authority (described on p. 84 of part II of the report of the 1948 Lambeth Conference), which is 'seen to be moral and spiritual, resting on the truth of the Gospel, and on a charity which is patient and willing to defer to the common mind'.

Thus it is evident that we, the Churches of the Anglican Communion understand ourselves to participate in the one, holy, catholic, and apostolic Church, worshipping to one true God, Father, Son, and Holy Spirit.

We profess the faith revealed uniquely in the Holy Scriptures and set forth in the Catholic creeds. Of this faith the central mystery is that of Jesus Christ himself, the Word made flesh, whom we proclaim to be the way, the truth, and the life. In the story of his life, death and resurrection, and ascension, we perceive, in a unique and irreplaceable way, the terms of God's utterly costly self-identification with the human condition, his victory over sin and death, and the hope of final redemption. We join with all Christian people in proclaiming in word and in deed this good news, which is the power of God unto salvation, and from it we draw our life, through the Holy Spirit, who directs and cleanses his Church.

This Conference desires in particular to reaffirm the central position which the ordered worship of the Church occupies in the distinctive basis of the Anglican Communion. This worship, itself a witness to the apostolic Gospel in word and sacrament, patterns and limits the diversity which has characterized Anglicanism from the first. It provides a framework in which the variety evident in Scripture itself may be interpreted. Furthermore, it brings the worshipper into the company of those who, from the earliest days, have offered a spiritual sacrifice to God.

The Churches of the Anglican Communion acknowledge under the guidance of the Holy Spirit, the Apostles' and the Nicene Creeds as 'the sufficient statement of the Christian faith' (Chicago–Lambeth Quadrilateral of 1888), as confessed and taught in the service books and catechisms of the Churches. The Communion desires to remain reticent about making any closer definition of the gracious mystery of God's reconciling act in Christ, and the loving presence of the Holy Spirit shed abroad in the hearts of Christian people. Instead, by a constant acknowledgement in worship of the source of all spiritual life, we seek to be led to 'a due sense of all [God's] mercies'. It is in this context that the Christian may grow to a fuller maturity in Christ, and be equipped for the loving and liberating service to God and his neighbour.

Accordingly, in order to find out what characterizes Anglican doctrine, the simplest way is to look at Anglican worship and deduce Anglican doctrine from it. It should be further noted that the recent adoption by almost all Anglican provinces of new forms of liturgy which clearly resemble each other in their main outlines in fact brings into prominence (even if this is not expressed in confessions and declarations) aspects of doctrine not previously given particular stress. Among these might be mentioned the congregation's part in celebrating the Eucharist, the responsibility of ministry laid on all Christians, and the setting of the death of Christ within the whole context of the creation, history of salvation, incarnation, resurrection, ascension, and outpouring of the Holy Spirit. We do not intend a 'confession' which will mark us off from other Christian communions; rather we desire a unity of doctrinal tradition sufficient to express our abiding will to live together and to worship together the one Lord of the one, holy, catholic, and apostolic Church.

B. Partners in Mission

The Partners in Mission programme has become a significant element in the life and mission of the Anglican Communion. We begin by acknowledging this fact with gratitude. The second meeting of the ACC in Dublin in 1973 initiated the method of joint consultation as one expression of partnership and we make special mention of the work of the ACC office and the Rev. David Chaplin in enabling no less than 24 consultations to take place so far.

The third meeting of the ACC at Trinidad in 1976 made an evaluation and appraisal of the PIM process which we strongly endorse. We urge all member Churches to study with fresh care this evaluation, together with the guidelines which have been prepared for the second round of PIM consultations. We support the proposal of a continuing process of joint consultation at three- to five-year intervals. In addition to the recommendations set out in resolution 17 of the Trinidad meeting of the ACC, we urge the following (see resolution 15 of this whole Lambeth Conference):

1. The consultation process is concerned with the meaning of mission as well as its implementation. This point is made clear in the Trinidad report (*ACC–3 Trinidad,* p. 57, para. 2(b) (ix)), but has not yet been widely received. PIM consultations may be weakened or confused by the failure to recognize that their purpose is to bring about a renewed obedience to mission and not simply to make an existing system efficient. We therefore recommend that each Province seek to educate Anglicans in the meaning of the PIM process and of the significant re-orientation of mission strategy which is involved.

2. One way of achieving this is to encourage the Church to experience the PIM principle at many levels of its life: e.g. between provinces in large national Churches, between dioceses, between a group of parishes, or between parochial and sector ministries.

3. We draw attention to the weakness of the ecumenical dimension in many past consultations and urge the correction of this in the future.

Anglicans in any place cannot undertake mission effectively without consulting and planning with fellow-Christians.

4. Churches should not be content with inviting partners only from those areas which share a natural or racial affinity with them. The insights of other cultures, and of various understandings of mission, are vital to growth in a true and balanced theology of mission, and to ensuring the possibility of a creative exchange of resources both personal and material.

5. Representatives of partner Churches do not always have long enough in the host Church and country before the consultation begins. We believe that a period of two weeks, or even longer, would be helpful and appropriate in most situations. Forward planning should allow invitations to be sent out well in advance.

6. We believe the PIM process can help all of us to catch the vision of an interdependent world as well as an interdependent Church. To this end we underline how essential it is that, where possible, the key secular issues should also be well presented in each consultation and by those in society who understand them best.

7. PIM has helped us develop the concept of sharing rather than of some giving and others receiving. Yet there is an ever-present danger of lapsing into the 'shopping list' way of thinking. At the same time we are sure that consultations should always contain the opportunity for the frank stating of specific needs.

8. Within the Anglican Communion as a whole, thought needs to be given to follow-up as well as co-ordination of response to PIM consultations. We recommend that the ACC gives particular attention to this matter.

C. The Gospel and stewardship

God himself is the almighty resource of the Church. Our feeble prayers are necessary but are only made effectual by being mingled with those of 'him who ever liveth to make intercession for us'. We believe that prayer and reliance upon the Holy Spirit must be the spiritual basis of any plan of action in the Church.

We claim that God has already given his people all the human and financial resources necessary to carry out his mission in the world. The problem persists that so many skills remain uncommitted and so much money 'remains firmly in the pockets of Church members'. A greater degree of realism about what sacrificial giving means, and a wider sharing of knowledge, skills, and resources is called for. People will give according to the measure of their love for God and understanding of the Gospel. We need to study motivation and encourage Christians to give and serve for the right reasons.

We therefore call on all members of the Churches of the Anglican Communion not only to recognize the duty and privilege of stewardship, but also to participate in the joy and fulfilment of giving with a cheerful and willing spirit. Giving must be planned, realistic, and sacrificial; but its spiritual source lies in the response of heart and mind to God's gratuitous and superabundant generosity in his creation, and in his redemption of mankind through Jesus Christ.

Stewardship teaching must, therefore, be regarded as an essential element in all Christian education in parishes and training institutions. The primary responsibility for stewardship teaching belongs to the bishop and the clergy.

We, therefore, urge all Anglicans, especially in the western world, to review their value systems so that life-styles may become related to necessities rather than affluence and consumerism. We commend the biblical principle of tithing, and call upon bishops to pledge themselves to accept it in order to give a lead to their clergy and people.

The scriptural injunction 'he who would be chief among you, let him be the servant of all' requires bishops to reject pretentious life-styles and by example to lead their clergy and people in the wise use of their personal resources and also those of the Church (see resolution 9).

D. Structures in the Anglican Communion

We recognize that the Lambeth Conference and the Anglican Consultative Council are separate bodies in the life of our Communion. There is no necessary structural relationship between the two, though the ACC was set up by the synods of member Churches on the recommendation of the Lambeth Conference 1968, which established its terms of reference.

The Lambeth Conference has always been a gathering of bishops brought together at the invitation of the Archbishop of Canterbury, to enable those called to exercise episcopal leadership to meet for mutual exchange and enrichment.

The ACC is a representative body of bishops, clergy, and laity, set up by the synods of the member Churches who each take their own synodical actions in respect of its decisions and recommendations.

The Archbishop of Canterbury, as president of both bodies, is a permanent link between the two, and the availability of the present Secretary General of the ACC, Bishop Howe, as Secretary of the Lambeth Conference of 1978, has been a further link.

We wish to express great appreciation of the value of Bishop Howe's work in helping Provinces and dioceses to keep in touch with one another.

We believe that it was wise to restrict the size of the ACC both on grounds of finance and to ensure its effectiveness as a consultative body. But this means that the representation of each Province is small and that those who are the delegates of the Churches must be very carefully selected. It is essential that they should know what their Church thinks on the subjects under discussion and that they should be in a position to report back fully. We welcome the appointment of a Communications Officer by the ACC and hope that he will be able to facilitate a two-way traffic between the ACC and the Provinces. He will be a member of a very small staff, but we feel it is important that the staff of the ACC should be known and trusted throughout the Communion and be seen to be responsible to all 25 member Churches.

We have noted that while the ACC looks to the Archbishop of Canterbury's Counsellors on Foreign Relations to handle relationships with the Roman Catholic Church, the Orthodox Churches, and certain others, its own staff handle other inter-Church relationships directly. The work of the CFR and that of the ACC should, in our opinion, be more closely co-ordinated, and we ask the ACC to take the initiative in seeking such co-ordination.

We have learnt with interest that the ACC secretariat has recently become more involved in helping to plan the tours undertaken by the Archbishop of Canterbury and we think it important that he should be seen to be making his visits on behalf of all the Churches of the Anglican Communion. While the diplomatic representatives of the countries concerned naturally wish to welcome him, such visits should be seen as being primarily to the leaders and people of the Churches. We hope that in the future the host Province will take a larger share in planning the programme for such visits.

We have noted that there have very occasionally been meetings of the primates of all the Provinces. Since such meetings are important for a Communion which is both episcopally led and synodically governed, we hope that such meetings will be held more often, perhaps in connection with meetings of the ACC.

One of the basic principles of Anglicanism is that no diocese or bishop should exist in isolation. In the past most isolated dioceses have been related to the See of Canterbury, the Archbishop of Canterbury has exercised metropolitical authority, and the bishops of such dioceses were related to him. With political changes and the union of Churches in recent years, a number of additional isolated dioceses have come into existence and a variety of patterns of exercising metropolitical authority have arisen. This situation has revealed that there is a lack of clarity about what metropolitical authority involves. We are glad to note that the ACC has taken the initiative in trying to clarify this concept in consultation with the Provinces of our Communion.

Since our Communion is a group of autonomous Provinces, and every network of relationships within it needs to be strengthened, we ask the ACC to encourage regional grouping of Provinces and to be ready to provide such groupings with help and advice.

We think it possible that the ACC might wish at some future date to hold an Anglican Congress (such as those held in 1954 and 1963), either on a worldwide or a regional basis. Nevertheless, we do not consider that such a Congress can ever take the place of either the Lambeth Conference or the ACC, and we should expect it to raise grave financial problems (see resolution 13).

We are confident that by the turn of the century, the role of the Archbishop of Canterbury as the acknowledged focus of unity of the 25 autonomous Churches of the Anglican Communion will make the international aspect of the appointment even more demanding both in time and leadership than it is at present. We recognize that this cannot but have implications for the Church of England and for the province and diocese of Canterbury.

We have learnt with interest of the revised arrangements for the nomination of a new Archbishop of Canterbury and have noted that the Secretary General of the ACC will be a member of the Appointment Commission. We are glad that other Provinces of the Anglican Communion will thus be able to make their views known through Bishop Howe or his successor.

We have noted that all Provinces but one (Papua New Guinea) are constituent members of the World Council of Churches and we recommend that the ACC secretariat should convene a meeting of all Anglican members attending a WCC Assembly or a Central Committee meeting in order that both the contribution of the Anglican Communion in formulating WCC policy and the informing of the Anglican Communion about such policy should be strengthened. We also hope that the ACC will help to recruit Anglican members of the WCC staff.

2. The Anglican Communion in the *oikoumene*

A. The World Council of Churches

The concern for Christian unity has never lessened in the WCC. We see this in the work of the Commission on Faith and Order, especially in its report 'One Baptism, One Eucharist and a Mutually Recognized Ministry'; we also see it in the WCC's growing relationship with the Roman Catholic Church. We hope that the time is not too far away when there will be full Roman Catholic participation in the WCC, as is now true in a number of national and regional Councils.

Representation from the 'younger Churches' has made it clear that for many of them the survival and freedom of their people must be a major concern. In the fellowship of the WCC their pleas have been heard, and there have been programmes of relief, resettlement, education, the struggle for justice and freedom, and the combating of racism. To many western Christians, the WCC seems very radical, but what they fail to understand is that the 'centre' has shifted dramatically with the influx of new Churches. And those Anglicans who complain about the policies and actions of the WCC need to be reminded that beloved members of our own Communion in the under-privileged areas of the world are among those who seek WCC help in their efforts to make life better for their people. The WCC is not 'they' doing something to 'us'. It is 'we' working with our own and others in ecumenical endeavours. As bishops of the Church, we have an obligation to know and understand what is being done, and to find ways of informing our people. The question to be faced also by all of us is: What structures and inter-relationships, involving national and local Councils and Churches, and our world-wide Anglican family as well as the WCC, can best serve the advance towards unity in each place and in all places? (See resolution 29.)

B. Our relations with other Churches

Developments within the Anglican world since the Bonn Agreement of 1931 have made it necessary for us to consider anew the types of eucharistic and ecclesial fellowship possible between Anglican and non-Anglican Churches. The concordat of inter-communion with the Old Catholics at that time has been followed by a series of similar agreements with other Churches. Some of those are based largely on the Bonn Agreement. Others are a result of Anglican dioceses entering into united Churches which desire to maintain a continued bond with the Anglican family.

We have been made aware of the sense of isolation felt by bishops now in united Churches that embrace former Anglican dioceses. Such isolation inhibits the fulfilment of the office of bishop to which a focus of the Church universal properly belongs. Therefore we are proposing that in future bishops from these Churches should be full members of any Lambeth Conference (see resolution 14).

It seems likely that in the next decade still more ecclesial families will be included in an expanding eucharistic fellowship with Anglican Churches. Some of these will be as the result of formal concordats or agreements, increasing the membership in what is known as the Wider Episcopal Fellowship. Others will simply be the result of Churches in a given region growing together in mission and ministry and at the table of the Lord. In such cases it is important to be flexible without compromising our basic principles upheld in the Lambeth Quadrilateral.

We received with thankfulness the report of the International Anglican–Lutheran Dialogue, authorized by the Lambeth Conference of 1968 in response to the invitation of the Executive Committee of the Lutheran World Federation. We have also heard with pleasure of the many new moves towards closer fellowship and co-operation of individual Lutheran and Anglican Churches in a number of parts of the world, such as the present conversations in Europe, America, and Tanzania (see resolution 31).

We welcome the setting up of conversations between the Anglican Communion and the World Alliance of Reformed Churches and we look forward to hearing of the progress of these conversations.

In addition to these officially recognized dialogues at the international level, we note the great variety of negotiations and conversations being carried on as Anglicans explore the possibilities for unity with other Christian Churches. The 'Ten Propositions' for a covenant between five Churches in England, the proposal for a United Church in Sri Lanka, new developments in the Consultation on Church Union in the United States, and others, are evidences of creative efforts being made to respond to our Lord's prayer 'that all may be one'.

We would encourage further discussions between Churches locally as well as internationally, and particularly urge the careful consideration of both current and future ecumenical studies by all Church members.

We note the negotiations now proceeding with the Lusitanian and Spanish Reformed Churches, which appear to fulfil the above characterization of the Churches in the Anglican Communion, and which are now seeking fuller participation in the life of the Anglican Communion as constituent Churches.

In this connection, we wish to recall resolution 63 of the Lambeth Conference of 1968 concerning parallel Anglican jurisdictions in Europe. Since a solution has not yet been found we urge that the positive efforts made so far be given greater emphasis. We hope that a pattern of fullest co-operation be worked out with other Churches, particularly those with whom we are in communion (see resolution 14 (2)).

We need to make evident and give expression to the large area of common ground that exists between us and other branches of the Christian family, in faith, order, and mission. This common ground is, perhaps, most crucial to the ongoing work of understanding and growth together at the parish level where differences have often been maximized. Steps therefore need to be taken with a greater degree of enthusiasm to correct this, and in this connection it is essential that the bishops of the Church be informed about and deeply involved in all of these ecumenical endeavours and developments. But if there is to be progress in Church unity, all members of the Church must be kept informed and involved in the national and local experiments and plans for union. Bishops need to accept responsibility for securing and disseminating information throughout their jurisdictions.

In connection with inter-Church relations, we have noted the need for consistent terminology describing varying types and degrees of unity, and definitions of ecclesial Communion. The present lack of clarity leads to confusion among Anglicans and non-Anglicans alike. We would like to ask the ACC to develop appropriate definitions of such terms as 'organic union', 'conciliar fellowship', 'full communion', 'inter-communion', and 'restricted inter-communion', and to make these definitions known to the member Churches for the sake of consistent usage (see resolution 30).

C. The Roman Catholic Church

The Lambeth Conference of 1968 recommended the setting up of a joint theological commission by the Anglican and Roman Catholic Communions. We therefore believe that Lambeth 1978 should evaluate the fruits of the Anglican–Roman Catholic International Commission's work, as found in the three Agreed Statements—on Eucharistic Doctrine (Windsor, 1971), Ministry and Ordination (Canterbury, 1973), and Authority in the Church (Venice, 1976).

Most of us assent fully to the Agreed Statements, but some would prefer to regard them simply as a basis for further discussion. Additional explications from ARCIC (at present under consideration by ARCIC) have helped to remove many of the doubts expressed. Areas of disagreement await further study between and within the two Churches, as well as by ARCIC itself.

We were concerned that the Churches should now be challenged to take further the process of seeking for unity. We believe that the way forward towards a closer sharing between our two Communions in life, worship, and mission, should be in the context of the Malta Report of 1967. This Report envisaged a process of 'unity by stages' and among its proposals are the following:

1. A common affirmation of faith in fundamental matters of belief. The achievement of this is reflected in the Common Declaration of Pope Paul VI and the Archbishop of Canterbury in April 1977 (see especially paragraph 2 of that Declaration).
2. Annual regional meetings of the bishops of the two Communions. Some of these have been taking place.
3. A whole series of consultations and reciprocal activities at all levels. In some regions there has been some progress in these.

We hope that the common faith expressed in the Agreed Statements will be a stimulus to growth into 'unity by stages' and to the implementation of those steps recommended in the Malta Report which have not yet been taken everywhere in our two Communions. We look forward to further steps towards a closer unity in the future (see resolution 33).

The problems associated with marriage between members of our two Communions continue to hinder inter-Church relations and progress towards unity. While we recognize that there has been an improved situation in some places as a result of the *Motu Proprio,* the general principles underlying the Roman Catholic position are unacceptable to Anglicans. Equality of conscience as between partners in respect of all aspects of their marriage (and in particular with regard to the baptism and religious upbringing of children) is something to be affirmed both for its own sake and for the sake of an improved relationship between the Churches (see resolution 34).

D. Orthodox Churches

We welcome the character and progress of the theological dialogue with the Orthodox Churches, and believe that the Moscow Agreed Statement of 1976 goes far to realize the hopes expressed at the Lambeth Conference of 1968. We note:

1. the international character of the talks;
2. their official character; and
3. their concern with the major doctrinal themes of the Christian faith.

Two world Christian families are learning to talk to each other from very different historical experiences. Too hasty a demand for practical results may threaten more fundamental achievements.

However, there is a need to bridge the gap between the official theological discussions and the fragmentary relationships between Anglican and Orthodox in different parts of the world. Much useful dialogue exists, e.g. between Anglican and Orthodox staff and students in universities, and also in parish situations where theological questions arise out of practical questions of shared Churches. We recommend that the present theological Commission should promote regional groups for theological dialogue, which would assist local groups in the handling of material such as the Moscow Agreed Statement, and bring up to the official Commission not only reactions to their work, but also theological issues arising out of local experience. In so many areas, e.g. the Middle East and Eastern Europe, we are all surrounded by greater numbers of people of other faiths and ideologies. The form and range of our dialogue have been dictated by internal Christian preoccupations, and the desire to reach reconciling formulae to clarify and resolve them. While we recognize that this characteristic of the present report is proper, and indeed commendable, we believe that there is urgent need to set these internal Christian themes of our debate in the much wider context of the contemporary world.

We take note of the message addressed directly to the Lambeth Conference by the special meeting of the Anglican–Orthodox Doctrinal Commission last month in Athens. We believe this illustrates;

1. the need to strengthen Church-to-Church communication between Anglicans and Orthodox;
2. the need to strengthen communication between the member Churches of the Anglican Communion and the theological commissions which represent them;

3. the need to state clearly that there are some decisions affecting Catholic faith and order which should not be taken independently by member Churches. It might be the responsibility of the Lambeth Conference, or some other authorized body, to indicate what these issues are.

A specific request has been made to the Lambeth Conference on the subject of the *Filioque* clause[1] in the Creed. The Lambeth Conference has had this subject on its agenda since 1888, and we believe that the recent history of debate about this in member Churches illustrates the need to strengthen the communications mentioned above.

The Anglican–Orthodox Joint Doctrinal Commission has proposed that:

1. because the original form of the Nicene Creed referred to the origin of the Holy Spirit from the Father;

2. because the *Filioque* clause was introduced into this Creed without the authority of an Ecumenical Council and without due regard for Catholic consent; and

3. because this Creed constitutes the public confession of faith by the People of God in the Eucharist.

the *Filioque* clause should not be included in this Creed. This is in accord with the recommendation of another Theological Commission, set up by the Archbishop of Canterbury, which reported in 1976.

Both Commissions stress that the recommendation is made on historical grounds which have important implications for ecumenism, collegiality, and authority. It would apply only to the Nicene Creed and not to other liturgical formulae. This leaves open a number of other theological questions, since the *Filioque* clause enshrines certain truths about the mission of the Holy Spirit in the world, as distinct from his origin.

In the light of the recommendations made by our theologians, and having regard to the fact that the *Filioque* has been omitted for similar reasons by the Old Catholic Church among others, and to the fact that the Roman Catholic Church permits its omission from the rites of the Uniate Churches and from the Latin rite in Greece, we believe that in subsequent revisions of the liturgy Anglicans should have the opportunity to recover the original form of the Creed (see resolution 35).

On the subject of the ordination of women to the priesthood, we believe that the Lambeth Conference should respect and take account of the deep feelings expressed by the Orthodox. However, our conversations were started in order that attention should be given to fundamental questions of

[1] In the Nicene Creed as used in the Western Churches, the Holy Spirit is said to proceed 'from the Father and the Son (in Latin, *filioque*)'. In the original version he is said to proceed 'from the Father' only.

doctrinal agreement and disagreement, and not simply to isolated questions such as inter-communion and the recognition of orders. We believe that our present situation is firmly within such declared understanding of the inclusive nature of the conversations, and therefore we hope that they will continue to be sustained by the full weight of Orthodox authority. Now that the Anglican Communion is trying to wrestle with difficult and divisive questions about the ministry of women in the Church, there is greater need than ever to examine along with the Orthodox fundamental theological beliefs about ministry, in the light of which alone responsible decisions can be reached. We have no doubt at all that the wisdom and experience of the Orthodox are needed and will be gladly heard in our Communion.

We are encouraged by the official statement made by the Ecumenical Patriarch, and other Orthodox leaders, that the dialogue should continue, and we welcome his statement that 'the points which unite us outnumber those which separate us Orthodox and Anglicans'. We believe that difficulties which arise in our relationships as Churches should not put a stop to discussions, but rather underline the need for a continuing dialogue on the fundamental doctrines of our faith, in the course of which both sides can listen to, and learn from, each other.

3. Evangelization and renewal

In our report we have now spoken of the inner life and external relations of the Anglican Communion. It remains to speak, however summarily, of two things which touch the heart of all Christendom, and not of our Church alone, viz. the proclamation of the good news of Jesus Christ, and the power of his Spirit to renew the Church in our time.

In paragraph 13 of his apostolic exhortation *Evangelii nuntiandi,* Pope Paul VI wrote:

> **Those who sincerely accept the Good News, through the power of this acceptance and of shared faith, therefore gather together in Jesus' name in order to seek together the Kingdom, build it up and live it. They make up a community which is in its turn evangelizing.**

How does such gathering together actually take place?

1. In Councils of Churches, from the international to the local level. We owe much valuable reflection on evangelism, for example, to the World Council of Churches. It is our hope that Councils everywhere will not be afraid to deal with deep spiritual concerns and will not confine themselves to the realm of the milder social issues.
2. In the setting of the world-wide evangelical movements and fellowships, we have been glad to note a growing convergence in understanding the need for evangelism between Evangelicals, 'ecumenicals', and Roman Catholics (compare with the above quotation from Pope Paul VI, many sayings from the Lausanne Report of 1974).

3. Most of all, in the local and informal coming together of those who have themselves accepted the Good News and seek to witness to it. The formation of lay groups, in places of work as well as of residence, is to be welcomed and encouraged. Such groups almost inevitably cross denominational frontiers.

There has recently been a tendency in many Churches to depreciate the importance of the preaching ministry, but we remain Churches of the word as well as of the sacraments, and the ministry of the word is a vital ingredient of effective evangelism. We should, therefore, wish to see serious attention given, by preachers and congregations alike, to biblical contemporary teaching.

Too often the Church remains insensitive to some of the deepest forms of expression known to humanity—those found in music, drama, and the arts—which can show dimensions of our faith additional to those of the spoken word. We hope they will be widely employed in God's service.

Again, we are constantly reminded that we live in the age of the mass media and their immense influence, whether for good or ill. To many people today, this is how the Good News will come, initially at any rate, if it comes at all. The skills required both for production and for the presentation of Christian truth (in a myriad of different ways) need to be recognized among the priorities of the Churches to-day. At the same time, personal encounter and personal teaching has not been superseded by the media, but should follow up their initial impact wherever possible.

To sum up: Since we have been commanded by our Lord to proclaim the news of salvation to all nations, and since there are over two billion persons in the world who need to know Christ crucified and risen, Anglicans are called upon to commit themselves afresh to the work of evangelization, in co-operation with their fellow-Christians of other Communions wherever possible.

Meanwhile—and long before our own seeking—the Holy Spirit has been manifesting his presence and power anew in the Church today. In various parts of the world, and not least where there has been severe pressure or threat of trouble, we have seen a kindling of true discipleship, evangelical zeal, and a growth both of numbers and spiritual power. Thus the 'renewal movements', including the charismatic movement, have become a feature of the life of many different Communions, our own included, and for this we thank God. Many of these movements are lay-directed, and express themselves in prayer groups, ministries of healing, Bible study, liturgical participation, and an acceptance of lay ministry in individual activities, as well as in our corporate life—for there is a new conviction that, as St Paul said, each one has received his gift from the Spirit. These congregations have been quickened, and the ecumenical movement has come alive in new ways through increased, though informal, local participation.

The history of such renewal movements, from the earliest Christian times, shows certain dangers inevitably accompanying the enthusiasm which they generate. There can be a spiritual pride which leads to sectarianism, often due to an understanding of the Spirit which is not fully trinitarian. Nevertheless, our chief desire, as a Communion, should be to receive, and know how to use, these 'manifold gifts of grace' (see resolution 7).

The recent experience of the charismatic movement gives but one example of the old tension in which humanity—not just the Church—has always lived, viz. that between authority and freedom. We may feel that tension with particular sharpness today, for pluralism and the questioning of authority are characteristic of much contemporary society. In their search for what is real and authentic, many people are questioning (if they have not already rejected) traditional patterns of belief, worship, and Christian morality. It is therefore inevitable that innovations and individual judgements which are counter to tradition should sometimes be considered as attributable to the guidance of the Holy Spirit. Others are doubtful of such claims, still holding strictly to the superior authority of the Body, and gravely suspect the judgements of individuals and small groups.

We believe that it is often the case that new ways of expressing the truth of the Gospel, or of ordering the ministry of the Church, need the test of time before we can truly discern the leading of the Holy Spirit. We must therefore wait upon the Spirit, calling for charity and forbearance, when confronted by differing convictions and practices within the one Body. Under God, this is the Anglican way at its best.

Seven searching questions

At the Hearing entitled 'The Anglican Communion and its Future' Archbishop E. W. Scott of Canada posed seven searching questions. These we leave as a spiritual check-list for our Churches in the years that lie immediately ahead.

1. Are we discovering, through our faith in Jesus Christ, resources which enable us to face the kind of realities to which Christian economists such as Barbara Ward and Charles Elliott call our attention, which provide us with both motivation and some sense of direction in seeking to respond to them?
2. Have we discovered, and can we share with others, insights which enable us to live with a sense of meaning and purpose in the midst of the urban, industrial, scientific, and technological society with which more and more of us are being confronted?

3. Are we finding in our faith, and can we help others find, the resources which enable us to face and live in the midst of the realities of racism, cultural tension and conflict, brutality and human degradation, and not to be destroyed by them but enabled to react back upon them with some degree of creativeness?

4. Are we discovering in our common loyalty to Jesus Christ the grounds of a community deep enough and strong enough to enable us to relate to each other honestly and frankly and without claiming moral superiority, no matter how complex or controversial the issue we face may be, without breaking the commitment to Jesus Christ and to each other?

5. Are we discovering the ability to uphold what we believe to be basic Christian values, and at the same time to minister with love and concern to those who have not been able to live up to the standards? And to do so in a way that does not create a sense of condemnation or rejection and seem primarily legalistic?

6. Are we discovering a depth of community which means that the needs of people in one part of the world call forth a response from people in other parts of the world which is both real and practical? Are we revealing such concern and response in relation to those who have been imprisoned or exiled for their faithfulness? Some bishops have been exiled. Can we respond, as a Communion, to their need?

7. Are we finding, and can we help others find, a faith that will enable us to live in hope, and with love?

A message to Crossroads, South Africa

The Conference heard of the plight of the black squatter families in the camp of 20,000 people known as Crossroads, within the Cape Town diocese of South Africa. Crossroads is to be demolished on the orders of the South African Government and the wives and children there are to be repatriated whilst their husbands and fathers will have to stay in single-sex hostels if they wish to retain their work and livelihood. Since there was to be a service at Crossroads on Sunday, 30th July and a simultaneous one, in solidarity, on the steps of the church of St Martin's-in-the-Fields in London, the Conference voted *nem. con.* on 28th July that the following message be sent to Crossroads and to St Martin's, to be read at the services:

We, the bishops of the world-wide Anglican Communion meeting in the eleventh Lambeth Conference, greet you, the people of Crossroads, in the Name of our Lord Jesus Christ.

We support your struggle for the right to a stable family life and pray that the authorities will not demolish your homes until they have provided you with adequate alternative homes at the place where the breadwinner now works.

Grace, peace and joy.
Your brothers in Christ.

The bishops of the Lambeth Conference;
Archbishop of Canterbury, President.

The Dean of Botswana

A statement by the Primates Committee

The Committee of Anglican Primates, meeting at the time of the Lambeth Conference, gives thanks for those priests who at this time are ministering Christ's love to the homeless and dispossessed in Southern Africa, and deplores the apartheid form of government which is producing this situation.

In particular, we express our dismay and protest against the recent unwarranted arrest and detention by the authorities of the Republic of South Africa of the Anglican Dean of Botswana, and others imprisoned and restricted because of their ministry to the dispossessed in their continuing anguish.

10th August 1978

Appendix

Some speeches made during the Conference

1. An abbreviated version of Professor John Macquarrie's introductory speech at the Hearing on 31st July on the ordination of women to the priesthood.

2. The speech made by Bishop Cyril Bowles, Bishop of Derby, on 10th August, introducing the debate on the ordination of women.

3. A speech on 'Authority in the Anglican Communion' made by the Archbishop of Canterbury on 7th August.

1. Professor John Macquarrie

The question of the ordination of women to the priesthood is one that has been debated in the Anglican Communion for a good many years. I do not intend to rehearse the arguments, for I think we are all familiar with them. I do want to say, however, that both sides have argued the case with skill and integrity, both sides deserve respect, and the question cannot be held to have been conclusively settled one way or the other.

But the question is no longer only an academic one about possibilities. Some branches of this Communion have already proceeded to the ordination of women. Female priests exist, and even those who would deny the ontological reality of women priests are not able to deny their empirical actuality. This fact complicates the issue considerably, for some Churches of our Communion are still at the stage of discussing whether they are going to ordain women, others that have ordained them are dealing with the problem of how most effectively to use their ministry, while a new set of problems arises concerning the relations between those Churches that have women priests and those that do not.

I have said that I do not intend to rehearse the familiar arguments for and against. Instead, I would like to do three things. First, to take a step back from the arguments, to try to sort them into categories, to try to subject the different categories to critical evaluation, and to ask how one recognizes the different categories and what weight attaches to each. Second, to explore the question of what we mean by a 'consensus'. How much agreement should there be before such a major innovation as the ordination of women is implemented? Obviously these two points are chiefly of interest to Churches which have not yet decided whether to ordain women. But since women priests are already a fact, there is a third group of problems. How, given that we are still far from a consensus and that opinion is deeply divided, do we arrange matters within individual Churches, within the Anglican Communion as a whole, and in our relations with other Communions?

First, then, there is the analysis and evaluation of arguments in those Churches which are still at the stage of considering the pros and cons of the case. Everyone wants to claim that his arguments are theological but every theology comes out of a particular historical situation and is therefore culturally and sociologically conditioned. This seems to me to put a question mark against many of the arguments which the defenders of a male priesthood draw from the New Testament. On the other hand, the sociological critique of theology itself needs to be criticized and it very rarely is. If every theology bears the traces of a sociological conditioning, it is equally true that every sociology has its implicit theology, or, better, ideology, that is to say, its value system in the light of which it selects and evaluates its facts. The sociological critique of theology demands to be corrected by the theological critique of sociology. It does seem to me that some of those who have been most forward in criticizing the tradition on the grounds of its cultural bias have themselves been operating in terms of an uncriticized secular ideology, characterized by egalitarianism, relativism, sometimes also an alleged need for confrontation—characteristics which are all very questionable from a Christian point of view. I make these points to show that although some Churches have already come to decisions on the question of women's ordination, the argument is by no means over and ought to be pursued in greater depth.

Next we come to the question of a consensus. It cannot mean everyone thinking alike. Theology is a dialectical science, so that every minority view has its elements of truth and justification. The majority view needs the constant stimulation and correction of the minority view if it is to remain alive and seek deeper truth. A measure of pluralism is today an acceptable and healthy state of affairs within the Church. But sheer pluralism would mean the dissolution of the Church. The liberty of pluralism is possible only because there are wide areas of agreement. This is especially the case where we are concerned not only with belief but practice. The ordination of women to the priesthood and episcopate is such a novel step that it does seem to me to demand a large measure of consensus if it is not to provoke very deep division and even schism. In practical terms, I should think such a consensus could be understood as the two-thirds majority required in many bodies for radical changes, and that this consensus should obtain severally among the bishops, clergy, and lay people. I believe also that where such a consensus is present, many of those who had previously opposed the change will accept that it represents the mind of the Church, perhaps even the leading of the

Holy Spirit, and will go along. Here one is obviously thinking of some particular national or regional Church, and in the first instance a consensus has to be sought within such a Church. But the question does arise whether on such an important and potentially divisive issue as the ordination of women to the priesthood, one should not look for a consensus beyond that of the national or regional Church. It is true of course that within the Anglican Communion, each constituent Church is autonomous. But I must confess that I am not much impressed with the idea of an autonomous Church. This is especially the case at a time when we hear a great deal of talk about collegiality, partnership, conciliarity, and so on. If there are not just empty words that are bandied about, if they stand for a real desire to share experience and decision-making, then each so-called autonomous Church ought to be in constant consultation with its sister Churches. On the particular matter with which we are concerned today, it would surely have been wise if individual Churches had deferred action until this Lambeth Conference of 1978.

I pass on now to our third problem or rather group of problems—those arising out of the fact that some Churches have exercised their autonomy and ordained women priests, so that within the Anglican Communion we now have Churches that have them and Churches that do not, within those Churches that have them there are those who accept their ministrations and those who do not, schism has taken place and new questions are being raised about Anglican relations with Rome and the Orthodox. How do we sort out these problems?

First of all, I think we have to get the problem into perspective. Most theologians would agree that in Christianity there is what has come to be called a hierarchy of truths, that is to say, there are some central doctrines which comprise the very heart of Christian faith, there are others which may be less central but are nevertheless moderately important and well attested, while there are others still which are more peripheral and about which there is some question as to whether or not they are implicates of the central truths. It seems to me quite clear—and I think I have perhaps shown in the earlier part of this paper—that the question of whether women can be priests belongs to this outer grey peripheral area. It is certainly not I would say a question by which Christian faith either stands or falls. Hence I do not think that the ordination of women priests in a Church is a sufficient ground for people to leave that Church and to set up a schismatic body. Anglicanism has always been a form of Church that can accommodate wide differences, and today even the Roman Catholic Church acknowledges the need for pluralism in those fringe areas where different theological opinions are possible and legitimate. In the past Anglicans may have disagreed about doctrine but have been fairly uniform in practice; for instance, there have been different doctrines of the episcopate, but episcopal ordination has been invariable. Now perhaps we have to consider some pluralisms of practice as well, in the development of women priests. Are those members of the Church who conscientiously believe that a woman cannot validly consecrate the Eucharist (and who can prove beyond doubt that such persons are mistaken?) to be forced either to go against their consciences or to leave the Church? On the other hand, we have equally to respect the consciences of those bishops and others who believe it their duty to recognize the genuineness of the call of certain women to priestly ministry. Surely it is possible for us to work out a *modus vivendi* in a spirit of reasonableness and mutual respect.

One has also to ask the question of how the existence of women priests in Anglican Churches will affect our relations with Churches outside our own Communion. The major difficulty will arise with Rome and the Orthodox. It will be sad indeed if the promising *rapprochement* between Rome and Canterbury is halted or slowed down by the ordination of women priests in Anglican Churches. This may very well happen, and I hope we all realize that we may be paying a very high price for what we are doing. Yet perhaps it won't happen, and here I would appeal to the generosity and understanding of the Roman brethren in particular. If indeed, as I have claimed, women in the priesthood is a genuinely disputed question belonging to that peripheral area where pluralism is legitimate, is it not possible for our two Communions to continue to grow together on the basis of the many things that they have in common, while respecting differences of discipline on matters which surely do not make or unmake a Church?

2. Bishop Cyril Bowles

In moving resolution 21, I speak as the chairman of the group which considered the ministry and ordination of women. We were a small and mixed group, like the rest, from different parts of our Anglican Communion. There were some of us who hold that the ordination of women is wrong and those also who believe that it is right. In spite of our differences we worked in the greatest amity. Not a single unkind or unfair word was spoken. There was no acrimony. Every member applied himself from the very beginning to secure agreement. There was no desire to gain victory for any particular point of view. The result was that we were able to make a unanimous report to our section. When the section discussed it they sent us back with suggestions for the amendment of our motion. We did extra work and returned with our recommendations. We were sent back again to reconsider one particular clause. After this work the resolution as a whole was accepted in the section with only seven people voting against it. We were trying to deal with the situation in which there already are women priests in some provinces, something like 150 in all. We did not examine the rights and wrongs of the particular issue. That was dealt with by the last

Lambeth Conference and the member Churches of the Anglican Communion must now work on that. Here the discussion could be sterile. We looked at our situation as it is with the two sharply opposed convictions.

In clause 1 of our resolution we attempted to state the position as it is. The problem for the Anglican Communion at this present time is stated in clause 3. There could not be in our discussion in our group a triumph of one view over the other and we made no attempt to decide the battle. Among ourselves we represented the problem. There were those, first, who believe that the doctrine that the priesthood must be male is part of the faith once delivered to the saints. There were those, secondly, who look on the ordination of women as St Peter looked on the Gentiles who had received the Holy Spirit: 'Who can forbid the laying-on of hands in ordination to these women who have received the Holy Spirit for ministry as well as we?' I belong to the latter group myself. Bishop Bill Folwell, who is to second the motion, belongs to the former. There is no possibility of resolving the conflict between these two views, except within one fellowship of faith. The Anglican Communion is such a fellowship of faith in God and so of trust between its members. It must set itself to be such a fellowship and remain so. Only so shall we be able to grow together into the truth. That is why clause 4 runs: 'the Conference affirms its commitment to the preservation of unity within and between all member Churches of the Anglican Communion'. This is in accordance with the teaching of the New Testament where the fellowship of the Spirit, the *koinonia,* is the place of spiritual insights. Unity is the gift of the Spirit, but it has to be maintained. Schism only occurs where people *will* schism instead of willing unity. Besides that, if the Anglican Communion were to break up, it would no longer be able to make any contribution to the larger unity of the Church. Our comprehensiveness must be made credible in action. That involves our holding together so that we may show the kind of unity that we have and can share with others. The preservation of unity demands particular actions. So clause 5a makes it clear that all member Churches must continue in Communion with one another. There must be no overt or concealed excommunication of dioceses or individuals.

Similarly clause 5b makes it clear in what it says that there must be no discrimination against people because of their views. People can feel isolated because they are part of a minority, but they must be helped to realize that they still belong to the fellowship. This may involve particular efforts to reconcile and heal. It may involve cost in both offering and accepting forgiveness. It may involve a conscience clause, as in the Church of Canada, which everyone, whatever his or her convictions, accepts. Within this setting of faith, of commitment to one another and the sustained will for unity, there must be further study, and there must be a continuing effort to see the ministry of women in its wholeness. That is the point of clause 5c. However few or many women may be ordained, the majority of women will have some other ministry. All Churches are involved in this and the Orthodox Churches, for example, make remarkable use of a wide ministry of women, but it is important that the subject of the ordination of women to the priesthood should be put in this larger setting. Actions and study will only be effective if there is general and wholehearted acceptance of one another by our member Churches. This matter is dealt with in clause 6a and 6b.

One particular expression of acceptance is mentioned in clause 6c. Some provinces or dioceses may not be able conscientiously to accept, even on a temporary basis, the ministry of women ordained elsewhere. Some may and, if so, a basis for this is recommended. First, it must be based on pastoral need which may be that not only of a parish, say, but also of a woman priest herself. But the clause is intended to make clear that the celebration of the Eucharist by a woman must never be used for the purposes of propaganda or demonstration. Section c(ii) makes the point that there must always be respect for people's consciences at every level and in all relationships.

Concerning clause 7, strong representations have been made to us by the Roman Catholic Church, the Orthodox Churches, and the Old Catholic Churches. It would be most discourteous, to say the least, merely to go our own way and say nothing. We must go our own way when truth and loyalty to our own Communion demand this, but we are engaged in dialogue with two of these groups and have full communion with the third. This clause is an attempt to avoid rebuff, to state our own position, and at the same time to show some humbleness of mind. Therefore, we say, first of all, in section (a) of clause 7 that we are not merely making the best of a bad job. We are doing something much more positive than that. Here is an inherent part of our Anglican inheritance, the holding together of diversity within a unity of faith and worship. This is not something that was invented at the time of the Reformation and developed in subsequent centuries. It is something to be found in the New Testament itself, Christians respecting one another, sharing a common life, and accepting also a diversity of conviction on sundry matters. Section (b) makes clear what is being thought about when we refer to the ordination of women to the priesthood. Whether we believe it is right or wrong, we are not introducing something new. Those who have been ordained have been ordained into the historic ministry of the Church as the Anglican Communion has received it. In section (c) of this clause we make it clear that we still want to learn. We do not possess all the answers, but so long as Churches are disunited something is lacking of the fullness of catholicity, of the measure of the stature of the fullness of Christ.

Clause 8 asks for the discussion to be put within the consideration of the wider theological issues of ministry and priesthood. This was a suggestion that was made at the Hearing and an important one. The ordination of women to the priesthood should not be considered as a subject in isolation.

This resolution as a whole is a compromise, but it is a compromise that expresses a most delicate balance, seeking to do full justice to the varied convictions in our Church. It is compromise, but the other word for compromise is reconciliation. 'Accept one another', St Paul says, 'as Christ accepted us, to the glory of God.' We have to express the kiss of peace on the levels of theology and ecclesiastical politics. It must be a sacramental action and not a mere social custom introduced into our liturgy. Christ accepted us, the unacceptable. We in the Anglican Communion over this issue, like the early Church facing the vast divide between Jew and Gentile, must accept one another however unacceptable our convictions or practice may be. This can have the Cross in it, as some in our group and section have already discovered, but this acceptance could be a point of creative growth in the whole life of the Anglican Communion.

3. The Archbishop of Canterbury

Brothers, I think many of you have been feeling during our last two weeks that a word needs to be said about the complex and difficult subject of authority in our Anglican Communion, and if you would allow me, I would like to say a word about that at this particular stage in our three weeks' work together.

We have been searching somewhat uneasily to find out where the centre of that authority is. Many of us have wrestled with that old one for many long years. Some of us, particularly the majority who have come to this Conference as their first Lambeth Conference, have only recently begun to wrestle with it.

May I say something about it which I hope may be of help in the coming days? There are those who would say perhaps that authority ought to be centred in the person of the Archbishop of Canterbury himself, but down the years the feeling against that has, I think rightly, been strong. It is not, I believe, of the genius of Anglicanism to have at its head someone who is papal or patriarchal, though that has been discussed many a time. Those of you who have been reading Alan Stephenson's *Anglicanism and the Lambeth Conferences* (which came out just in time for this Conference) may recall that on pages 100f. of that book there is a reference to the fact that the then Bishop of Albany in the year 1897 wrote to Davidson about it. Frederick Temple in that year took the chair of the Lambeth Conference but Davidson was a figure of power even before he came to Canterbury. Davidson in replying to Bishop Doane said: 'That anything in the nature of a Canterbury *Patriarchate* will receive the support of the Conference I do not for a moment believe. Some would wish for it, but they will be few. On the other hand the idea of some central tribunal of reference, for disputes on doctrinal or even disciplinary questions, has got a firm hold on the minds of very many, perhaps I ought to say of *most* of the Colonial and Missionary Bishops.'

Is the answer then to rest with the Lambeth Conference? Again the answer has been, and again I think rightly, no. For, so far, we have insisted on saying that we are not a legislative body. We are what our title implies—a conference, a conferring body. We may sense a consensus and that is very important, but we do not legislate.

Is the central authority of the Anglican Communion, then, to rest with the Anglican Consultative Council? Again I believe the answer is no. This, though a synodical body, consisting of bishops, priests, and laity, is not representative enough—anything like representative enough—of the whole world-wide 65 or 70 million of us. About the relationship of the Lambeth Conference to the Anglican Consultative Council, Bishop John Howe will speak to us in a moment.

What then, fourthly, of a Doctrinal Commission? I believe the Communion needs one, but again I cannot see this as being the authoritative council of the Anglican Communion, for it will deal with only one part, a very important part, of the work of our Communion—that is to say, the doctrinal part. But the pastoral and the practical aspects will not be its primary concern. It will be an advisory Commission again.

Well, so far, so negatively. What then? Now it seems to me that we, as a Communion, are feeling the tension, which many member Churches feel, between episcopal guidance and synodical government. I rejoice that we are an episcopal Church and I hope that we shall never lose sight of that. But we are also coming to grips with the fact of synodical government and haven't entirely as yet learned how best to live to the mutual comfort and help one of the other in this 'marriage'. Here is a tension, and I believe such a tension is good for our Communion, as it is good for our provinces and for our dioceses. For you only get music out of a violin string when it is taut—you only get a groan when there is no tension.

I do not think there is a quick or easy answer to the question 'Where is authority to be found?' Nor do I think it is of the genius of Anglicanism to define too rigidly, though there is always, on the part of some of us, a craving for a rigid neatness. But I am coming to believe that the way forward in the coming year—and it may be a slow process—will be along two lines: first, to have meetings of the primates of the Communion reasonably often, for leisurely thought, prayer, and deep consultation. There have been such meetings, but on very informal and rare bases. I believe they should be held perhaps as frequently as once in two years. But if that meeting now on some fairly regular basis is to be fruitful, those primates would have to come to such meetings well informed with a knowledge of the mind and will of their brothers whom they represent. Then they would be channels through which the voice of the member Churches would be heard, and real interchange of mind and will and heart could take place. That's the first thing.

The second line, I think, on which we might well make progress would be to see to it that that body of primates, as they meet, should be in the very closest and most intimate contact with the Anglican Consultative Council. And this, I believe, will only take place when we have a Communications Officer who can lift something of the burden from the present Secretary General who has done the work so splendidly, with all his other burdens, hitherto. But I think it of ultimate importance that ACC and the primates meeting regularly should be kept in the closest possible liaison.

Thus we might achieve over the years increasing consultation and maintain close links between the trio of bishops, priests, and laity, and between the 25 member Churches of our Communion. We should, I believe, come to a common mind on main issues and we should avoid the danger of one Church, or two or three Churches, going off on their own without due consultation—at the same time maintaining the independence of the member Churches themselves. Such a liaison between the Churches in the persons of the primates and the ACC representing synodical government would be greatly facilitated, as I have already said, by the appointment of a Communications Officer.

I believe that on lines something like these—without a rigidity which would be foreign to our tradition—we should move towards a maturity in the exercise of authority which would be to the good of our Communion as a whole and might well be the means through us of our making a contribution to the whole Catholic Church of God.

Index